CW01647313

A History of the Canberra Raiders

2024 Edition

Matthew Geddes

First published in Australia in 2017 by
Parallel Partners
PO Box 190
Crookwell NSW 2583

Geddes, Matthew

A History of the Canberra Raiders
ISBN 978-1-68419-017-1

Cover Stars: Canberra Raiders celebrate their 1994 premiership victory

Produced by Parallel Partners Books

Introduction

Canberra and surround districts had along relationship with rugby league long before the introduction of the Raiders to the New South Wales Rugby League premiership in 1982.

Teams formed around Canberra, Yass, Queanbeyan and Goulburn shortly after the game started in Australia in 1908. By 1928 the Federal Capital Territory league was formed, and was absorbed into the Group 8 competition in 1932.

The regional competition was suspended in 1941 due to the Second World War, but resumed in 1946. Two years later Canberra centre or five-eighth Johnny Hawke was picked in Australia's Kangaroo Tour squad. In 1949 he moved to Sydney and captained St George to a premiership victory.

In 1974 the competition was split into two groups, with teams around Goulburn playing in Group 8; and Canberra and districts playing for the Molonglo Shield in Group 19.

In 1982, the Canberra Raiders were granted entry into the NSWRL competition. Former international Don Furner was appointed coach, and journey forward David Grant was the club's first captain.

1982

In 1981, the New South Wales Rugby League decided to expand the boundaries of the competition for the first time since Cronulla and Penrith entered in 1967. As Sydney's population expanded, teams from Wollongong and Campbelltown were expected to be granted entry.

Although the Illawarra Steelers were successful in gaining entry to represent Wollongong and surrounding districts; Campbelltown was overlooked. The Sydney clubs were reluctant about the inclusion of Canberra; but a guarantee of being compensated for travel costs swayed the objections; and the Raiders were born.

Don Furner had represented Australia on the 1956 Kangaroo Tour while playing in Toowoomba. He made his name as a coach at Queanbeyan; although he had a brief stint in Sydney at Eastern Suburbs. The Roosters made the Grand Final in 1972 under Furner's coaching. He returned to Queanbeyan the following year, and was a natural choice to be the first choice of the Raiders.

David Grant came from Forbes in western New South Wales to join South Sydney in 1976. After a successful rookie season Grant was signed by Easts, but struggled to make first grade. He joined Balmain in 1978, and played with the Tigers for four seasons during a lead period for the club. A clever ball player, Grant was a key signing for Canberra in 1982, and was appointed captain.

The Canberra forward pack of 1982 relied on young forwards Jon Hardy, Mick Tilse and Carl Frommel; but did include former Queensland hooker Jay Hoffman; and tough Wests forward John McLeod.

The key signing in the backs was North Sydney utility Alan Smith; who had represented Queensland in the inaugural State of Origin match in 1980.

Young utility Craig Bellamy joined the Raiders from St George; as did Balmain five-eighth Lloyd Martin and veteran Penrith halfback Terry Wickey. They also had a promising local halfback in Chris O'Sullivan.

Canberra faced South Sydney at Redfern Oval in their first match on February 27, 1982. The first Raiders team was Sam Vucago, Chris O'Grady, Peter McGrath, Frank Roddy, Steve O'Callaghan, Lloyd Martin, Gerry De La Cruz, Carl Frommel, Jon Hardy, John McLeod, David Grant, Jay Hoffman and Jeff Simons. The reserves were Mick Tilse and Scott Dudman.

De La Cruz scored the first try in the history of the club, but Souths were too strong, scoring seven tries in a 37-7 victory. Winger Mark Ross scored a hat trick for the Rabbitohs.

Canberra played their first home match at Seiffert Oval in Queanbeyan against Western Suburbs. A crowd of over 6700 turned up to watch their new team. Young five-eighth Terry Lamb scored two of Wests' seven tries as they ran out winners 33-4. The young Raiders side was quickly finding out just how tough it was to play in the best rugby league competition in the world.

North Sydney ran in seven tries to one in a 27-5 win at North Sydney Oval in round three; with Smith and Wickey making their debuts for the new club.

Canberra were competitive in their next home match against Canterbury, but ultimately went down 22-9. In round five they gave St George a scare before halfback Steve Morris scored two tries to give the Dragons a 13-4 win.

Craig Bellamy and Chris O'Sullivan made their debuts for Canberra in the round six clash against Manly at Seiffert Oval. They went down 23-13.

In round seven, Canberra ran into a red hot Parramatta side at Belmore. Parramatta were the reigning premiers, and included internationals Mick

Cronin, Ray Price, Ron Hilditch and Bob O'Reilly; and young backs Eric Grothe, Brett Kenny, Steve Ella and Peter Sterling who would all go on to play for Australia by the end of the year. Eric Grothe crossed for four tries, and Mick Cronin scored 27 points as the Eels crushed Canberra 54-3.

Canberra returned home humiliated, but were buoyed when a crowd of close to 10,000 attended Seiffert to watch their side take on 1981 runners up Newtown. The Jets were expected to make light work of Canberra, and scored three tries to two. However, three goals from Steve O'Callaghan gave Canberra a 12-11 win to secure the club's first ever victory. John McLeod and Chris O'Sullivan scored the tries for the Raiders.

Canberra came back to earth in round nine when they faced fellow newcomers Illawarra in Wollongong. The Steelers ran in nine tries in a 45-0 thrashing.

The Raiders conceded ten tries against Cronulla the following week, including a hat trick to fullback Mick Mullane. The Sharks ran out winners 44-5.

In round eleven, Canberra went to Leichhardt Oval for the first time, and were smashed 35-0 by Balmain. Rookie forward Wayne Pearce scored a double for the Tigers.

The goal kicking of former New South Wales fullback Kevin Dann proved the difference as Penrith beat Canberra 27-19 at Seiffert. Both sides scored five tries in the match. Young winger Angel Marina became the first Canberra player to score two tries in a match.

Canberra again suffered a heavy loss in round thirteen. They went to the Sports Ground, and let in thirteen tries in a 55-15 loss to Easts. Kevin Hastings scored a hat trick for the Roosters.

Balmain ventured to Canberra the following week. The result was much closer than the bout at Leichhardt, but the Tigers still ran out winners by 29-18, scoring seven tries.

Round fifteen saw Canberra win their second match of the season. They scored five tries to four in a 23-18 win over Souths at Seiffert Oval.

The next week saw Canberra again heavily beaten. Steve Broughton scored four tries, and former Australian lock Jim Leis crossed for a hat trick as Wests ran out winners 40-8.

Canberra went down 23-9 to North Sydney in round seventeen; and conceded eight tries in a 34-16 loss to Canterbury the following week.

In a major upset, Canberra defeated St George by 25-22 at Seiffert Oval in round nineteen. Angel Marina scored a hat trick for the Raiders, while goal kicking forward Gary Britt scored thirteen points.

A rampaging Manly side scored thirteen tries in a 61-20 win over Canberra in round twenty. Mike Eden kicked eleven goals for the Sea Eagles; and only two tries from Chris O'Sullivan saved Canberra from suffering their heaviest loss.

Canberra went down 37-5 to Parramatta the following week; and in round 22 were smashed at the hands of Newtown by 42-5. The Jets scored ten tries in the victory.

In round 23, Canberra won for the fourth time; beating Illawarra 26-19 at Seiffert Oval, scoring six tries to three.

A 34-5 loss to Cronulla ensured Canberra would finish their debut season with the wooden spoon. They were beaten 42-5 by lowly Penrith in the second last round; and ended their year with a 35-5 loss to Easts.

Canberra finished their first season with four wins and 22 losses. While their rookie backline lacked the attacking flair of the top sides, there was an obvious need for an improvement in defence, as the Raiders conceded more than thirty points per game.

Young forward Jon Hardy was the only player to appear in all 26 games for Canberra in their debut season. Utility back Peter McGrath was their top scorer with 41, just ahead of Chris O'Sullivan on 37.

O'Sullivan was also the club's top try scorer with eleven; ahead of the consistent Craig Bellamy with nine, and Angel Marina on eight.

1983

Canberra went on a major recruiting drive for their second season. They signed former test winger Terry Fahey, goal kicking centre Ron Giteau, Newtown's try scoring winger Ray Blacklock and former Balmain and Newtown fullback Allan McMahon to strongly bolster their backline.

The Raiders secured the services of Cairns forward Sam Backo, and was joined in the pack by Crookwell local junior Ashley Gilbert, and Balmain veteran Gary Spears.

Chris O'Sullivan, Steve O'Callaghan and Craig Bellamy became regular first graders, while David Grant, John McLeod, Jon Hardy and Jay Hoffman gave experience to the pack.

Canberra went into their first match against Penrith at Seiffert Oval full of confidence, with Fahey, Giteau, McMahon, Blacklock, Spears and former Balmain utility back Percy Knight making their debuts.

Penrith halfback Henry Foster was the surprise packet of the match; crossing for a hat trick as the Panthers ran out winners 46-22 in an entertaining match.

Canberra faced 1982 premiers Parramatta at Belmore in round two. Neil Hunt scored three of Parramatta's eight tries in a 46-16 win, which saw Canberra's defence again being seriously questioned.

In round three, Canberra broke through for their first win of the season; beating Norths 32-10 at Seiffert. McMahon scored a double for the Raiders.

Canberra scored three tries to two in their round four match against Souths. A field goal from replacement back Ken Wright gave Souths a 17-16 victory. Sam Backo made his first grade debut in the match.

Terry Fahey was at his bulldozing best on the wing for Canberra in round five. He scored three tries in an unstoppable display as the Raiders beat Wests 30-22.

The following week Canberra travelled to Sydney to play Cronulla, and moved within a win of the top five with an upset 24-8 win. It was the first time Canberra had won two matches in a row.

In round seven Illawarra scored seven tries to three in a 38-24 win at Seiffert; but the Raiders remained two points short of the top five in a close competition.

Consecutive 24-14 losses to premiership heavyweights Canterbury and Manly saw Canberra drop back to eleventh on the table by the end of round nine.

The club Terry Fahey to injury during this period, diminishing their attack. They lost 30-6 to Easts in round ten; and followed up with a 30-18 loss to Balmain.

Canberra dropped to equal last on the ladder in round twelve when they were beaten 43-30 by St George at Kogarah. Veteran centre Steve Rogers scored seventeen points for the Dragons.

Canberra turned the halfway mark of the competition with a 31-12 win over Newtown. The Raiders scored five tries to two, and Ron Giteau finished the game with fifteen points.

Steve O'Callaghan scored three tries and Ron Giteau kicked seven goals for Canberra in their 34-22 win over Illawarra at Wollongong in round fourteen.

Craig Bellamy scored a double in Canberra's 28-24 loss to Penrith; but the following week the club had the greatest win in their short history.

At Seiffert Oval, Canberra defeated premiers Parramatta 8-0. Ron Giteau scored the only try of the match in the biggest upset of the season.

Canberra fell 20-6 to Norths the following week, and followed up with an 18-8 home loss to South Sydney. Their failure to win the closer matches saw them relinquish any chance of challenging for the finals.

In round nineteen, Canberra defeated Wests 24-16 on the back of two tries from Terry Fahey. It was the first time the Raiders had beaten any side twice during a season.

Canberra beat Cronulla 22-14; but were smashed by Canterbury in round 21 by 43-16. The Bulldogs scored eight tries to three in the win.

Canberra travelled to Brookvale in round 22 to take on competition leaders Manly. The Sea Eagles were pushed to the limit, but got home 18-12 thanks to the goal kicking of veteran fullback Graham Eadie.

The Raiders had one of their best results in the following round when they thrashed Easts 36-8 at Seiffert. Canberra scored six tries to one, including a double to Chris O'Sullivan.

The next week Canberra came back to earth when they were smashed 40-8 by Balmain. They went down 28-14 to St George, before going down in the last round of the season to Newtown by 9-6 at Henson Park. It turned out to be the last time Newtown would play in the top tier competition.

Canberra finished the season in tenth place with nine wins. Ron Giteau was the club's top point scorer with 193. Terry Fahey was the top try scorer for the season with eleven; one ahead of Chris O'Sullivan and Ashley Gilbert. O'Sullivan and Giteau played all 26 matches during the season.

1984

Canberra were much quieter in the player market for the 1984 season. With Newtown folding, the Raiders picked up utility back Ron Sigsworth and back rower Dean Lance, who would later captain the club. Clever halfback Ivan Henjak joined the club for St George, and young wingers Bill Walker and Matthew Corkery made their first grade debuts.

Canberra opened the season with an 18-14 win over Cronulla at Endeavour Field. Ron Giteau scored two tries and finished the match with fourteen points.

The Raiders made it two from two with a 22-12 win over Wests to become an unlikely equal leader of the competition. O'Sullivan scored two tries in the win.

Canberra lost 32-8 to North Sydney in round three, with the Bears running in five tries. Fullback Wayne Portlock finished the match with sixteen points.

The Raiders bounced back in round four with a 29-4 home win over South Sydney. They scored five tries to one in the victory to move back into the top five.

The demise of Newtown meant the necessity of a bye in the competition. Canberra enjoyed the week off in round five; but fell out of the top five when Peter Sterling scored a double in a 19-6 win the following week.

Canberra snuck home 12-8 against St George in round seven; and moved up to equal second spot on the ladder with a 14-10 win over Illawarra the following week.

Terry Fahey scored three tries and Ron Giteau kicked eight goals as Canberra smashed Easts by 44-12 at Seiffert in round nine.

In round ten, Canberra went to Brookvale to play top of the table Manly. The Sea Eagles were too strong, scoring five tries to one in a 28-10 victory.

Canberra went down 14-12 at home against Balmain the following week, and were on the verge of dropping out of the top five. The dropped to seventh after going down 28-10 against Penrith in round twelve.

At the halfway mark of the competition, Canberra were in fifth place on percentages after beating Canterbury 18-14. Craig Bellamy scored a double for the Raiders.

Canberra moved up to fourth place in round fourteen following their 38-14 home win over Cronulla. Craig Bellamy scored two of the Raiders' seven tries.

The Raiders fell out of the top of over the next two weeks after going down 16-6 to Souths and 17-14 to Norths. A 26-12 win over Wests in round seventeen saw them join Manly and Penrith in equal fifth place.

Canberra moved back into fourth spot with the round eighteen bye, and the following week a late try from Matthew Corkery gave them an upset 14-10 win over Parramatta.

Canberra then lost their next two matches to put their finals chances in jeopardy. They went down 15-2 to high fliers St George before losing 14-8 to Illawarra.

In round 22 Canberra snuck home 10-4 against the second last placed Easts thanks to the goal kicking of Ron Giteau. The win left the Raiders in sixth spot with four rounds to play.

Canberra beat Manly for the first time in round 23. They scored three tries to two in a 16-12 win to join the Sea Eagles in equal fourth spot.

A 39-12 loss to Balmain at Leichhardt Oval saw Canberra again fall out of the top five; but a hat trick from Chris O'Sullivan set up a 30-10 win over Penrith in the second last round to keep their chances alive.

Canberra were smashed 36-0 by minor premiers Canterbury at Belmore in the final round of the season. Losses to Penrith, Illawarra and Balmain saw Canberra finish in equal fifth spot with Souths.

For the first time in their brief history, Canberra played a finals qualifying match on the Tuesday after the final round, at the Sydney Cricket Ground.

Their side for the match was Ron Sigsworth, Mick Aldous, Ron Giteau, Craig Bellamy, Bill Walker, Ivan Henjak, Chris O'Sullivan, Dean Lance, Nigel Wilson, Ashley Gilbert, David Grant, Jay Hoffman and Gary Spears.

Canberra were overwhelmed by the occasion, and were defeated 23-4 by the Rabbitohs. Souths went on to beat Manly in the semi-final a few days later before being knocked out by St George. Canterbury defeated Parramatta in the Grand Final.

Ron Giteau was again the top scorer for Canberra with 163. Craig Bellamy topped the try scoring list with ten; one ahead of Chris O'Sullivan.

1985

After coming within a win of making the finals in 1984, Canberra relied heavily on the same squad for the new season. Journeyman forwards Brett Atkins and Terry Regan joined the club, as did Manly backs Michael Blake and Phil Carey. Young winger Chris Kinna became a regular first grader, and Great Britain hooker Kevin Beardmore had a brief stint with the club. Terry Fahey missed the entire season through injury.

Canberra opened their 1985 campaign with a 34-24 win over Illawarra at Seiffert. Craig Bellamy and Ivan Henjak both scored doubles, and Ron Giteau kicked seven goals.

Parramatta proved too strong for Canberra in their round two encounter. Mick Cronin kicked eight goals in the 36-22 win.

Bellamy again scored a double as Canberra defeated North Sydney 28-20; and a 26-14 win over Souths in round four consolidated the Raiders' place in the top five.

Veteran five-eighth Tony Trudgett scored a double as Penrith ran in seven tries in a 38-8 win over Canberra in round six in a major upset.

The Raiders were smashed 32-12 by Cronulla the following week, but recovered to beat last placed Wests 44-12 at Seiffert in round eight. Rookie winger Chris Kinna scored two of Canberra's seven tries, while Ron Giteau kicked eight goals.

Canberra's inconsistency continued with a 26-2 loss to Canterbury and a 20-20 draw against Manly. They went down 16-14 to Easts in round ten to be well outside the top five.

A tight 13-10 loss to Balmain followed before two tries and sixteen points from Ron Giteau set up a 20-10 victory over St George in Newcastle.

Canberra had the bye in round thirteen, but remained three points short of the top five at the midway point of the season.

Two tries from Craig Bellamy helped Canberra to a 31-22 win over last placed Illawarra in Wollongong in round fourteen.

The Raiders went down 24-10 to Parramatta the following week; but unleashed their beat attack against North Sydney, scoring seven tries in a 42-12 win in front of a paltry crowd of just over 1400.

The goal kicking of Ron Giteau got Canberra home 17-10 over Souths in round seventeen, which saw the Raiders move to within a win of the top five.

A 28-22 loss to Penrith followed by an 18-16 loss tı Cronulla put a severe dent in Canberra's finals chances. A 12-12 draw against Wests in round twenty, and a 28-16 loss to Canterbury all but ended their campaign.

Canberra lost 17-2 to Manly at Brookvale in round 22, leaving the club needing to win all of their remaining games to have a chance of making the finals.

Those chances came to a final end the following week when the Raiders were beaten 24-6 by Easts at Seiffert Oval.

With nothing but pride to play for, Canberra went down 30-12 to Balmain before suffering a humiliating 50-6 thrashing at the hands of St George. It was the eighth match in a row without a win for the Raiders, who finished the season in tenth spot after a last round bye. St George went on to make the Grand Final, but were beaten 7-6 by Canterbury.

Ron Giteau was again Canberra's leading point scorer with 167. Craig Bellamy topped the try scoring list with eleven; three ahead of Chris Kinna.

After a promising start to the season, Canberra needed to reassess after going without a win in their final eight matches.

1986

Canberra pulled off the biggest signing coup in the club's history in 1986 when they attracted Queensland and Australian centre Mal Meninga.

Meninga was joined by fellow Queenslanders Steve Walters, Gary Belcher and Gary Coyne, who would all go on to become legends of the club.

Veteran winger John Ferguson joined the club from Easts. A prolific try scorer, Ferguson had represented Australia in 1985, and had played for Newtown in the 1981 Grand Final.

Terry Fahey returned from injury; and Gilbert, Bellamy, O'Sullivan, Henjak, Backo, Lance, Hoffman and Carey again formed the nucleus of the side. Ron Giteau and Gary Spears were restricted to a handful of matches, and retired at the end of the season. Rookie wingers Kinna and Corkery played second fiddle to the international pairing of Fahey and Ferguson.

Canberra ventured to Brookvale Oval to play Manly in the opening round of the 1986 season. Mal Cochrane kicked six goals for the Sea Eagles in a 20-12 win in front of a crowd of just over 3000.

Ashley Gilbert scored two tries for Canberra in their second round clash against Balmain, but seven goals from Ross Conlon saw the Tigers run out winners by 26-20.

Canberra lost 22-10 to Illawarra in round three; but broke through for their first win of the season by beating Cronulla 26-12 at Seiffert Oval the following week.

The Raiders slumped to the bottom of the table in round five after going down 16-6 to Wests at Lidcombe Oval. A 22-16 loss to Penrith the following week kept them there.

Canberra went down 27-10 to Easts in round seven; and questions began to be asked how a team with half a dozen current representative players could be in last place.

The Raiders began to answer their critics in round eight by thrashing Norths 32-6. Gary Belcher scored two of Canberra's five tries.

The team had close losses to top contenders over the next two rounds; going down 14-8 to Canterbury, and 10-8 to Souths.

Canberra had the bye in round eleven, but the break did them no favours, as they went down by 28-18 to Parramatta the next week.

Five penalty goals from Mal Meninga helped Canberra to a 10-7 win over St George in round thirteen. They turned the halfway mark of the competition in equal last place with Cronulla.

Canberra put in a strong effort in their round fourteen match against manly at Seiffert Oval, and were only beaten by the brilliance of Manly back Phil Blake. The Sea Eagles ran out winners 25-18.

The Raiders lost their next match, 26-10 to Balmain, before beating Illawarra 26-12 at Seiffert Oval.

After going down 18-4 to Cronulla; Canberra smashed Wests 38-6; running in seven tries. The win saw the Raiders join Illawarra in equal last spot.

Canberra beat Penrith 20-4 in round nineteen to move away from the bottom of the ladder; and followed up with a 32-8 smashing of Easts in game where Mal Meninga kicked eight goals.

The Raiders were comprehensively beaten in their next two matches. They went down 31-10 to Norths and 32-14 to Canterbury to slip back to equal last spot with Illawarra.

Canberra lost their next match 11-6 to Souths, but a round 24 bye kept them from falling to last spot, despite Illawarra's narrow win over Penrith.

In round 25, Canberra caused the boilover of the season when they defeated top of the table

Parramatta 19-12 at Seiffert Oval. Ashely Gilbert scored a double for the Raiders.

Canberra finished a disappointing season with an 18-18 draw against St George at the Sydney Cricket Ground. They ended the year in eleventh place.

Parramatta recovered from their shock loss to finish the season as minor premiers, and controversially beat Canterbury 4-2 in the Grand Final to secure their fourth premiership.

Mal Meninga was Canberra's top point scorer in his first season with the club. He notched up 143 points, and represented the club at the end of the year by making his second Kangaroo Tour.

Terry Fahey was the top try scorer for the club with twelve; one ahead of Gary Belcher. Belcher joined Meninga on the Kangaroo Tour.

At the end of the season, Canberra decided to pursue an innovative dual head coaching structure for the following season. Queensland coach Wayne Bennett, who had mentored Meninga and Belcher at Brisbane Souths, joined Don Furner at the Raiders as they looked to make the finals for the first time.

1987

As well as securing the services of Wayne Bennett as co-coach in 1987, Canberra lured fellow Queenslanders Kevin Walter sand Peter Jackson to the club. New Zealand test front row forward Brent Todd joined the Raiders, and local juniors Glenn Lazarus and Laurie Daley made their first grade debuts during the season. Dean Lance was appointed captain of the club for the 1987 season.

Chris O'Sullivan scored two tries for Canberra in their 19-2 win over Cronulla at Seiffert Oval in the opening round. They had the bye in round two, and a 29-16 away win over Illawarra the next week had the Raiders leading the competition.

Canberra lost 10-8 to North Sydney at Seiffert in an upset in round four. They bounced back with a 22-14 win over St George at the Sydney Cricket Ground.

In round six, Balmain travelled to Canberra, and both sides scored three tries in the match. The goal kicking of Ross Conlon helped the Tigers kept home 26-18 to move to the top of the table.

Canberra dropped to fifth spot, but in a tight competition went back up to third by beating a struggling Penrith side 11-4. Matthew Corkery scored both tries in the match.

Canberra found their best form in round eight, running in eight tries in a 46-11 home win over Wests. Mal Meninga scored a hat trick and kicked seven goals to finish the match with a personal haul of 26 points.

The next week, Canberra led 22-0 at halftime in their match against Parramatta. The Eels rallied to score 30 unanswered points in the second half; highlighting inconsistencies in the Raiders, who remained in a four way share of second spot.

On a rainy Seiffert Oval, Canberra's hopes suffered a blow when Mal Meninga broke his arm in a match against Manly. Canberra fell to fifth spot after going down 18-10.

Veteran winger Peter Mortimer scored two tries for Canterbury in their 23-4 win over the Raiders; as they started to adjust to playing without Meninga. They fell out of the top five; and struggled to beat Souths 6-2 in a tryless match in round twelve.

Canberra lost 21-6 to Easts before smashing Cronulla 32-6 in an upset at Endeavour Field. The victory saw the Raiders move up to equal fifth spot.

After enjoying a week off with the bye; Canberra started the road to the finals with a 22-15 win over Illawarra. Ivan Henjak moved into the centres, and Kevin Walters was playing halfback. Gary Belcher had taken over the kicking duties in Meninga's continued absence.

In round seventeen, Chris O'Sullivan scored a double for the Raiders in their 18-12 win over Norths at North Sydney Oval. The win saw Canberra move into equal third spot with Balmain and Souths.

A 22-5 win over St George followed, but Canberra's premiership credentials were called into question when they lost 28-0 to Balmain at Leichhardt Oval in round nineteen.

Canberra faced Penrith and Wests over the next two weeks. Both sides were in equal last place, and proved little trouble for the Raiders. They beat Penrith 24-6 and Wests 30-12; but then lost 20-4 at home to Parramatta to place their finals chances in jeopardy.

In round 23 Canberra faced an under strength Manly at Brookvale Oval. The Sea Eagles were missing key attacking players Cliff Lyons, Michael O'Connor, Des Hasler, Noel Cleal and Dale Shearer. Both sides scored three tries, but a penalty goal from Mal Cochrane helped Manly to a 20-18 win.

Canberra kept their tenuous place in the top five by defeating Canterbury 22-4 at Seiffert; scoring five tries to one. Henjak had switched to halfback, with Walters now playing in the centres.

The Raiders secured their spot in the finals with an upset 26-2 win over Souths at Redfern Oval in the second last round. They gained momentum with a 22-18 win over the high flying Easts in the final round, thanks to two tries from Gary Belcher. Losses to Balmain and Souths saw Canberra finish in third place.

In their first finals match, Canberra faced Easts in front of more than 15,000 people at the Sydney Cricket Ground. The Raiders went into the match confident after beating the Roosters in the final round of the season.

The team for Canberra's first finals appearance was Gary Belcher, Chris Kinna, Ivan Henjak, Peter Jackson, Matthew Corkery, Chris O'Sullivan, Kevin Walters, Dean Lance, Gary Coyne, Ashley Gilbert, Sam Backo, Steve Walters and Brent Todd. The reserves were Terry Regan, Phil Carey and Laurie Daley.

Easts' captain Hugh McGahan scored two tries to lead the club to a 25-16 victory. The clubs were locked at 12-12 at halftime before the experience of Steve Morris, Tony Melrose and Tony Rampling helped the Roosters home.

Canberra faced South Sydney in an elimination semi-final the following week. The club focused their attack towards rookie winger Steve Mavin; and had scored three tries by the midway point of the first half. The Raiders led 28-6 at halftime, and the game was as good as over. The Raiders finished with eight tries, including a double to Chris O'Sullivan in the 46-12 win. Gary Belcher finished the match with eighteen points.

Canberra celebrated their first finals victory with the news that inspirational leader Mal Meninga would be available for the final against Easts.

Meninga scored a crucial try in the first half of his comeback to keep the teams level 14-14 at halftime. Steve Morris put Easts ahead with a try before Canberra unleashed an unstoppable attacking force to run out winners 32-24. Gary Coyne was the star, scoring two tries.

Canberra had qualified for the Grand Final for the first time. They played Manly, who were the best team all season, and had beaten the Raiders in both of their encounters during the year.

Manly were unstoppable in attack in the first half, with British forward Kevin Ward and five-eighth Cliff Lyons at their peak. Only handling errors at crucial times prevented Manly from scoring several tries in the first half as Lyons especially cut Canberra's defence to ribbons. Lyons scored the only try of the first half to give the Sea Eagles a 6-0 lead.

Manly went ahead 8-0 shortly after the break after a schoolboy offside error. Michael O'Connor scored from a Dale Shearer kick to put Manly up 14-0 midway through the second half.

Both sides traded penalty goals before Chris O'Sullivan scored Canberra's lone try to get the scoreline back to 16-8. Another penalty goal from O'Connor ended the scoring at 18-8, with the champion Manly centre finishing the match with fourteen points.

It was a heartbreaking end to the season for the Raiders, who had battled to keep their finals chances alive during Meninga's absence. The campaign saw Kevin Walters become a genuine first grader. He would go on to represent Australia for several years.

The Canberra side for the Grand Final was Gary Belcher, Chris Kinna, Mal Meninga, Peter Jackson, Matthew Corkery, Chris O'Sullivan, Ivan Henjak, Dean Lance, Gary Coyne, Ashley Gilbert, Sam Backo, Steve Walters and Brent Todd. Kevin Walters and Terry Regan were the reserves.

Gary Belcher was the club's top scorer for the season with 96; just three ahead of Mal Meninga. Matthew Corkery was the top try scorer with fourteen; three ahead of Chris O'Sullivan.

Don Furner resigned from the coaching role at the end of the season to concentrate on his role as Australian coach full time. Furner had coached the national side on an undefeated Kangaroo Tour in 1986.

Wayne Bennett also left the coaching position to become the inaugural coach of the newly appointed Brisbane Broncos club. Penrith coach Tim Sheens was brought to the club to build on the success of the 1987 squad.

1988

Tim Sheens inherited the bulk of the 1987 Grand Final side, with only retiring reserve forward Terry Regan unavailable. The club had a crop of young players coming through the ranks headed by Laurie Daley and Glenn Lazarus, who had experienced finals football in 1987. Lock forward Brad Clyde also impressed in his rookie season. Veteran winger John Ferguson was back in the side after recovering from a season ending injury in 1987.

Canberra began their campaign with a solid 28-8 win over Illawarra at Seiffert Oval. The Raiders scored four tries to one, and Gary Belcher kicked six goals. Mal Meninga missed the match, and Laurie Daley started for the first time. Veterans Mitch Brennan and Brian Battese also played for Canberra in the win.

In round two John Ferguson scored a double as Canberra ran in six tries on their way to a 34-10 belting of St George at Belmore. Ferguson again crossed for two tries in the round three 34-6 thrashing of South Sydney.

The round four clash between Canberra and Canterbury saw both sides go into the match undefeated. Canterbury scored four tries to three to go to the top of the table with a 22-17 win. Ashley Gilbert scored a double for the Raiders.

Canberra bounced back in round four with a 38-20 win over Cronulla in an entertaining match that produced eight tries. John Ferguson scored his third double for the season, while Belcher kicked nine goals.

Ferguson kept on scoring in round five scoring two of Canberra's seven tries in a 40-4 thumping of Easts. Laurie Daley also crossed for two tries, while Gary Belcher finished the match with sixteen points.

Canberra move back into an equal share of the competition lead in round seven by annihilating the newly promoted Gold Coast by 50-6. John Ferguson scored four tries, and Ashley Gilbert crossed for a hat trick.

The Raiders came back to earth the following week when veteran utility Paul Taylor scored four tries for Parramatta in a 40-12 victory.

Canberra went back to equal first place by beating Wests 30-16 at Campbelltown. Laurie Daley scored two of the Raiders' six tries.

Just three points separated the top ten teams by the end of round ten. Canberra stayed equal first despite going down 20-12 to North Sydney at Seiffert.

Canberra played Brisbane for the first time in round eleven. The Broncos; equal competition leaders with Canberra, went into the match without their captain Wally Lewis. The Raiders had rugby convert Ricky Stuart on the bench. Gary Belcher scored two tries and twenty points as Canberra ran out 36-16 winners to stay on top of the table.

The Raiders dropped back to second spot after losing 16-10 to Penrith; and fell to fourth place when Cliff Lyons scored three tries in Manly's 26-20 victory.

Kevin Walters returned to the starting line up in round fourteen, replacing an injured Laurie Daley. He scored two tries as Canberra defeated Balmain 39-15 at Leichhardt Oval.

Round fifteen saw Canberra play Newcastle for the first time. Mal Meninga made his return for the Raiders, while Laurie Daley returned to the side at fullback with Gary Belcher unavailable. Meninga scored a try and kicked five goals in his comeback to help Canberra to a comfortable 30-12 victory.

Belcher returned to the line-up the following week, while Ricky Stuart was at halfback. Kevin Walters joined Meninga in the centres. Stuart scored two of Canberra's six tries in a 31-22 win over Illawarra in Wollongong.

Mal Meninga and Ricky Stuart both scored two tries for Canberra in their 24-8 win over St George in round seventeen. The win saw the Raiders return to a share of the competition lead as just two points separated the top seven teams with just five rounds to play.

Gary Belcher scored two of Canberra's seven tries as they belted Souths 35-2 at the Sydney Football Stadium in round eighteen. The following week saw a top of the table clash between Canberra and Canterbury. The Bulldogs won 23-16 which saw the

Raiders fall to fourth spot. To make matters worse, Mal Meninga suffered another broken arm injury.

Canberra's finals chanced were placed in jeopardy when they were smashed 32-10 by Cronulla at Endeavour Field in round twenty.

The next week Canberra fielded a make shift side as Daley joined Meninga on the sidelines. Brad Clyde and Kevin Walters played centre as the Raiders got home 26-18.

The Raiders went into their last round clash against Gold Coast locked in a four way tie for fourth spot. Brad Clyde scored two tries from centre to help Canberra to a 24-4 victory over the last placed Seagulls. The win saw the Raiders bump Penrith out of third place.

Canberra played Canterbury in the major semi-final. The Bulldogs had won both clashes earlier in the season. The Raiders were again without Meninga and Daley.

Ashley Gilbert scored Canberra's only try of the first half, as they fell behind 16-6 at halftime. John Ferguson scored shortly after the break, and when Peter Jackson scored a fine individual try, the scored were locked at 18-18. A Terry Lamb field goal was all that separated the teams at fulltime as the Bulldogs ran out winners 19-18.

Laurie Daley returned from injury for the elimination semi-final against Balmain, with Brad Clyde playing from the bench. The match was played in rain and hail, and Peter Jackson scored the only try of the first half to give Canberra a 6-2 lead at the break.

In the second half, Ellery Hanley and Gary Freeman scored tries for Balmain to give the Tigers a 14-6 victory.

It was a disappointing end to the season for Canberra. They had missed Mal Meninga for most of the season; although he did recover to play in Australia's victorious World Cup final against New Zealand at the end of the year.

The rise of Laurie Daley, Brad Clyde, Ricky Stuart and Glenn Lazarus promised the future of Canberra would be bright. Queenslanders Gary Belcher, Gary Coyne and Steve Walters provided experience; although Peter Jackson and Sam Backo returned to Queensland at the end of the 1988 season.

Evergreen winger John Ferguson was the club's and the competition's top try scorer in 1988 with twenty. Gary Belcher was Canberra's top scorer with 218; which was enough to finish the year as the season's leading point scorer.

1989

Canberra lost Sam Backo and Peter Jackson at the end of the 1988 season. Young outside backs Mark Bell and Matthew Wood compensated for Jackson; while former Cronulla forward Craig Dimond joined the club. The Raiders again began the season without their captain, Mal Meninga, who had broken his arm for a fourth time in the World Cup final victory against New Zealand.

The Raiders faced 1988 minor premiers Cronulla at Endeavour Field in the opening round of the 1989 season. The Sharks were looking to overcome the disappointment of crashing out the finals, and started with a comprehensive 32-14 win on the back of sixteen points from Alan Wilson.

When Canberra went down 17-2 to South Sydney at Seiffert Oval in round two; the Raiders were languishing in last place on the ladder.

A Ricky Stuart field goal was enough to get Canberra home 9-8 over Easts to register their first win of the season. They started to get back to their best football the following week; beating Gold Coast 24-0 thanks to sixteen points from Laurie Daley.

Canberra moved into the top five for the first time in 1989 by thrashing premiers Canterbury 34-4 at

Seiffert Oval. Chris O'Sullivan scored two tries for the Raiders, as did Laurie Daley, who finished the game with 22 points.

The Raiders annihilated the winless Illawarra 44-8 in round six to move up to third place. Winger Phil Carey crossed for four tries. Mal Meninga made another comeback from the bench, and kicked two goals.

The Raiders were unstoppable in their 42-4 win over St George at Seiffert Oval. John Ferguson scored two of Canberra's seven tries. The next week they snuck home 12-10 against an under-performing Manly side at Brookvale Oval.

Canberra were at full strength for the first time in round nine; and ran in eight tries in a 41-16 win over Parramatta. Laurie Daley and Ricky Stuart both scored doubles.

In a major upset, Canberra went down 10-6 to Newcastle in round ten. They stayed in equal third place, four points behind competition leaders Brisbane and Souths. A 16-6 loss to Penrith the following week saw the Raiders drop to fourth spot at the halfway mark of the competition.

Canberra bounced back in round twelve when Brad Clyde scored two of their five tries in a 27-6 win over Brisbane. The following week they suffered an upset 25-22 loss to Wests which left them four points adrift of the top three.

Canberra beat a struggling North Sydney 14-5 before three consecutive losses saw them drop out of the top five. The Raiders lost 18-12 at home to Balmain; 22-16 to Cronulla, and 22-12 to premiership leaders South Sydney. The string of losses left Canberra in a three way tie in seventh spot with just five rounds to play.

The Raiders welcomed back Mal Meninga for their round eighteen clash against Easts. The Raiders snuck home 14-10 to keep their finals chances alive.

Gary Belcher scored two of Canberra's seven tries in their 42-18 win over Gold Coast in round nineteen. The result saw the Raiders move back into the top five; equal with a fading Brisbane.

In round twenty, Canberra and Canterbury clashed in the first premiership match ever played in Perth. Canberra all but ended the Bulldogs' season with a gutsy 18-14 win on the back of two tries from Laurie Daley.

After beating Illawarra 16-6 in the second last round, Canberra was locked in a three way tie for fourth place alongside Brisbane and Cronulla.

The Raiders travelled to Kogarah to play a disappointing St George in the final round. A win would secure a top five spot, while a loss had the potential for ending their season.

Gary Belcher was outstanding for the Raiders, scoring a hat trick as Canberra ran out comfortable winners by 30-16. It was enough to secure fourth spot on the table.

Canberra had to wait until the following Tuesday to see who they would play in the minor preliminary semi-final. Cronulla demolished Brisbane 38-14 in a playoff for fifth spot to play their third match in a week against the Raiders.

The Sharks started the match strongly, but fatigue eventually set in and Canberra ran out winners by 31-10. The Raiders scored six tries to one in the victory.

Canberra played Penrith the following week in the minor semi-final. Panthers coached produced a selection surprise when he replaced the veteran premiership winner Chris Mortimer with local rookie Brad Fittler.

The Raiders scored two tries against the run of play to open up a 10-2 lead, but Penrith hit back with two tries of their own to lead 12-10 early in the second half.

Replacements Paul Martin and Kevin Walters scored late tries, and Ricky Stuart kicked a field goal to wrap up a tough 27-18 victory for the Raiders.

Canberra faced South Sydney in the final. The Rabbitohs had been the best team all season, but had unexpectedly been beaten 20-10 by Balmain in their semi-final.

Gary Belcher and Steve Walters scored in the opening minutes and it looked as though Canberra would cruise to an easy victory. However, Souths fought back, and by halftime the match was level at 12-12.

Chris O'Sullivan and Mario Fenech traded tries early in the second half, but a series of penalties against the Rabbitohs allowed Mal Meninga to kick the Raiders in front. Late tries to Gary Belcher and Glenn Lazarus secured a 32-16 win for Canberra.

The 1989 Grand Final is widely recognised as one of the best premiership deciders of all time. Canberra had come from the bottom half of the finals draw to play the 1988 runners up Balmain. A capacity crowd of 40,000 filled the Sydney Football Stadium.

Early in the match, Balmain winger James Grant pounced on a wayward pass from Canberra prop Brent Todd, and outpaced the defence to score the opening try of the match.

The second try was one of the best seen in Grand Finals. Balmain's goal kicking British winger Andy Currier made a break and kicked infield for a rampaging Paul Sironen to score under the posts. Balmain went to the halftime break with a 12-2 lead, and looked set to make up for their 1988 Grand Final loss to Canterbury.

Canberra stayed in the contest with committed defence in the second half, and when Gary Belcher scored midway through the half, the Raiders were back in the game. Balmain had a chance to wrap up the game, but Michael Neil and Wayne Pearce both missed their opportunities. Ben Elias also missed a field goal, which ricocheted off the crossbar.

Balmain coach Warren Ryan, in his sixth Grand Final, decided to replace key forwards Steve Roach and Paul Sironen with proven defenders Kevin Hardwick and Mick Pobjie in an attempt to stifle the Canberra attack.

Canberra continued to throw everything at the Balmain defence, and in the final minutes Chris O'Sullivan hoisted a bomb which was gathered by Laurie Daley. Daley threw the ball to veteran winger John Ferguson who stepped inside the cover defence to score an unlikely try. Mal

Meninga converted, and at full time the score was 14-14.

With the match going into extra time, the move by Ryan to replace his two strike forwards was seen as a tactical error. Interchange players were not allowed at the time, and Roach and Sironen watched the rest of the game from the sidelines. It is a somewhat unfair criticism of Ryan, as Balmain needed defensive players during the final minutes of regulation time.

Balmain's international fullback Garry Jack spilled a kick near his line, and from the ensuing scrum Chris O'Sullivan kicked a field goal to give Canberra the lead 15-14.

With just two minutes remaining and the premiership hanging in the balance, unheralded replacement forward Steve Jackson undertook a regulation hit up twenty metres out from the Balmain line.

Jackson resembled a pinball as he bounced off desperate defenders on his way to crashing over for one of the most memorable of Grand Final tries. The Canberra players' emotions spilled over as they realised the try would give them victory in the Grand Final by 19-14.

Captain Mal Meninga, who had overcome an incredible number of setbacks to lead Canberra to victory described the victory as better than playing for Queensland or Australia.

It was a triumph for coach Tim Sheens, who had previously guided Penrith into their first finals appearance. He had guided the Raiders to their first premiership just eight years into their existence.

Lock forward Brad Clyde received the Clive Churchill for being the best player in the match. Clyde has progressed in leaps and bounds during the season, and was touted as a future Australian captain.

Laurie Daley was Canberra's top point scorer in 1989, finishing the season with 118; ahead of Gary Belcher on 82. Belcher was the club's and the competition's top try scorer with seventeen; one ahead of Daley.

1990

Fresh from their inaugural premiership win in 1989, Canberra went into the new season as competition favourites. They were helped during the season by having Mal Meninga and Gary Belcher fully fit; however utility back Kevin Walters left the club to play with Brisbane. The Raiders continued to unveil some impressive young forwards, such as Nigel Gaffey and David Barnhill. Hooker Wayne Collins was proving to be a more than capable backup for Steve Walters, and young outside back Brett Mullins made his first grade debut during the season. The Raiders had every reason to be confident.

Canberra also had a new home in 1990. They moved from the Queanbeyan based Seiffert Oval to a more centrally located Bruce Stadium. More than 22,000 fans packed the ground to watch their champions play St George in the opening round of the season. The Raiders started their premiership defence with a five tries to one 26-10 win over the Dragons.

The Raiders followed up with an 18-4 win over Illawarra in Wollongong; but were upset 6-2 at Bruce Stadium by Canterbury in round three. The Raiders' attack again faltered in an 8-7 loss to Cronulla.

Normal services were restored in the best possible manner in round five when Canberra scored a staggering twelve tries in a 66-4 annihilation of Easts. Mal Meninga scored a club record five tries and 38 points; while John Ferguson crossed for a hat trick against his former club.

Canberra beat Gold Coast 14-6 the following week; before turning on the attack again in a 48-14 round seven win over Souths. Mark Bell and Brad Clyde each scored two tries, and Meninga notched up eighteen points in the win which saw the Raiders move to within a point of the competition lead.

In their first meeting since the 1989 Grand Final, Canberra shut out Balmain 14-0 in a tough round encounter at Bruce Stadium.

The following week they returned to Perth for a match against Manly. Gary Belcher scored a double as the Raiders scored five tries to two in a 29-12 win.

Canberra went to the top of the table in round ten by beating Newcastle 27-21. John Ferguson scored two tries. The Raiders replaced Canterbury on top after the Bulldogs went down 24-4 to Balmain.

The Raiders stayed on top of the table at the midway point of the season, despite going down 17-8 to Parramatta. They stayed a point ahead of

Brisbane, Canterbury and Penrith; who in turn were just a point ahead of Cronulla, Balmain and Norths in one of the tightest ever competitions.

Laurie Daley scored twice in Canberra's 26-22 win over Wests in round twelve. They stayed on top with a six tries to two 33-10 thumping of Norths at North Sydney Oval the following week.

The match of the week in round fourteen saw top of the table Canberra travel to Brisbane. More than 32,000 fans packed Lang Park to see the Broncos displace Canberra at the top of the table with a 22-20 victory; helped by tries by former Raiders Peter Jackson and Kevin Walters.

Canberra dropped to fourth place after being smashed 23-2 by Penrith; but rallied to beat St George 28-12 at Kogarah in round sixteen to move back into the top three.

After a forgettable 8-8 draw against Illawarra; Canberra beat Canterbury 28-20 at Belmore thanks to two tries from veteran winger Phil Carey.

Two tries from Chris O'Sullivan helped Canberra to a 24-10 win over Cronulla in round nineteen. The win saw the Raiders move up to second spot; and all but ended the Sharks' chances of making the finals.

By the end of round twenty, Canberra, Brisbane and Penrith shared the competition lead; a point ahead of Balmain with two rounds to go.

The Raiders defeated Easts 26-10; and grabbed their spot at the top of the table when Penrith bear Brisbane 18-2. Canberra had by far the superior for and against of the three clubs.

All three clubs won their round 21 clashes; and all secured a spot in the top three after Balmain went down to Parramatta. Phil Carey scored two of Canberra's five tries in their 30-6 win over Gold Coast.

Canberra wrapped up the minor premiership with a 48-0 thumping of South Sydney at the Sydney Football Stadium in the final round. The match marked Brett Mullins' first game for the Raiders. Paul Martin, Glenn Lazarus and Ricky Stuart all scored doubles, and Mal Meninga scored 16 points.

Canberra had won the minor premiership for the first time. They enjoyed a week off after finishing ahead of Brisbane on percentages; but would face the third placed Penrith in their major semi-final after the Panthers beat the Broncos 26-16.

The Raiders went into the match with Phil Carey alongside Mal Meninga in the centres, and Laurie Daley at lock, after Brad Clyde had earlier suffered a season ending injury which rules him out of the 1990 Kangaroo Tour.

Laurie Daley scored Canberra's only try of the first half as they went to the break behind 8-6. A try from Glenn Lazarus midway through the second half put Canberra ahead for the first time; but two penalty goals from Penrith halfback Greg Alexander saw the match finish at 12-12.

Despite being refreshed from the break, Canberra were run over by Penrith in extra time. Tries to Alexander, Brad Fittler and veteran hooker Royce Simmons gave Penrith a 30-12 victory, and saw the Panthers into their first Grand Final.

Canberra regrouped to take on Brisbane in the final. The Broncos had edged out Manly 12-4 to advance, and welcomed the return of Wally Lewis from injury.

The Raiders moved Daley back to the centres, and promoted young forward Nigel Gaffey to the starting line-up.

Winger Paul Martin scored two first half tries, and mal Meninga crossed for one to set up a 16-0 halftime lead for Canberra. When Meninga crossed for his second shortly after the break, the Raiders moved to an unassailable 22-0 lead.

Phil Carey scored a late try for Canberra before towering fullback Paul Hauff crossed for Brisbane's only points of the match. Canberra won 32-4 to advance to their third Grand Final in four years.

Apart from Brad Clyde, Canberra went into the premiership decider at full strength. Veterans Phil Carey and Craig Bellamy were named on the bench.

Penrith, coached by Canberra coach Tim Sheens' former teammate Phil Gould, had exciting forwards John Cartwright and Mark Geyer, as well as the veteran Chris Mortimer. Their attack centred on Brad Fittler and Australian halfback Greg Alexander.

Halfback Ricky Stuart set up Canberra's first two tries to give his side a 12-0 lead. John Ferguson scored the first, before Laurie Daley crossed as Penrith looked shell shocked in the opening stages of their first premiership decider.

Brad Fittler scored for Penrith to bring the scoreline back to 12-6 at halftime. Panthers' winger Paul Smith crossed shortly after the break to cut the lead to 12-10 to ensure an exciting finish to the match.

Young replacement back Matthew Wood capitalised on a great backline move to score a try for Canberra to put them ahead 18-10. Greg

Alexander scored a late try, but it wasn't enough. Canberra had won their second premiership with an 18-14 victory. Ricky Stuart won the Clive Churchill Medal.

John Ferguson and Dean Lance announced their retirements at the end of the season. Chris O'Sullivan went to England to finish his career, but returned to the club for a handful of matches in 1992.

Mal Meninga was named captain of the Australian Kangaroo Tour squad after Wally Lewis was unable to pass a fitness test. Meninga was joined in the squad by his Canberra teammates Gary Belcher, Ricky Stuart, Laurie Daley and Glenn Lazarus.

Meninga was Canberra's and the competition's top point scorer in 1990 with 212. He was also the top try scorer for the club and competition with seventeen.

1991

Canberra went into the 1991 season without club stalwarts Dean Lance, Chris O'Sullivan and John Ferguson. They were well placed to replace them with Nigel Gaffey, David Barnhill, Mark Bell and Matthew Wood assuming more responsibility at the club. The Raiders signed Manly forward Glenn Ryan and Balmain utility Scott Gale. Bill Mullins started to make his mark on the competition, and was joined in the backline by rookie Jason Croker.

Canberra began their premiership defence with a shock 11-6 loss to North Sydney. Centre Peter Jackson scored a try and a field goal for the Bears against his former club.

The Raiders bounced back in emphatic style in round two, trouncing Parramatta 48-10 at Bruce Stadium. Mal Meninga and Matthew Wood both scored doubles as Canberra ran in ten tries.

Canberra went into their round three match against Brisbane at Lang Park without stars Gary Belcher and Brad Clyde. The Broncos proved too strong, scoring five tries to two in a 26-12 victory.

The Raiders narrowly beat Gold Coast 20-18 in round four before suffering a shock 24-12 loss to Wests at Campbelltown in round five.

The premiers sank to a new low in round six when they were humiliated 46-12 by Manly at Bruce Stadium. Sea Eagles fullback Matthew Ridge finished the match with 26 points.

The Raiders made several changed to their side for their next clash, against St George at Kogarah.

Scott Gale moved to fullback, and Brett Mullins and Jason Croker were selected on the wings. Brad Clyde returned from injury on the bench. Canberra scored five tries to two in a 28-12 victory to get their season back on track.

The following week Mal Meninga and Ricky Stuart both scored doubles for Canberra as they beat Cronulla 22-6 to move within a win of the top five.

Canberra beat Canterbury 18-16 in round nine; but inconsistency proved to be their weakness, as they went down 22-14 to South Sydney.

In their first meeting since the 1990 Grand Final, Canberra faced Penrith at Brice Stadium in round eleven. The Panthers were missing Greg Alexander, Royce Simmons, Brad Fittler, Mark Geyer and John Cartwright; and were no match for the premiers who ran out 20-0 winners.

Canberra lost 19-12 to Illawarra in Wollongong the following week. The Steelers were in the top five at the time. In round thirteen mal Meninga scored sixteen points for the Raiders in their 28-16 win over Newcastle which kept them in touch with the top five.

A 22-14 loss to Easts the following week saw Canberra drop to tenth place. They had just eight weeks to rescue their title defence.

In round fifteen, Canberra showed their best form, running in seven tries to two in a 36-16 win over Balmain at Leichhardt Oval. Matthew Wood and Jason Croker scored doubles for the Raiders.

Wood again scored a double as Canberra beat North Sydney 20-4 at Bruce Stadium to move back to within a point of the top five.

Canberra beat Parramatta 16-2 before going down 18-8 to Brisbane at Bruce Stadium to be three points outside of the top five with four games to play.

The Raiders beat Gold Coast 16-10 to keep their finals hopes alive; and joined St George in equal fifth place in round twenty by beating Wests 36-8.

Canberra snuck back into fifth spot after St George drew 12-12 with Norths in the second last round, and the Raiders beat Manly 14-13 at Brookvale Oval. Canberra scored three tries to one in the win.

The Raiders faced St George at Bruce Stadium in the final round. Canberra were in fifth place; just a point ahead of St George and Canterbury. A win would secure their spot in the finals, but a loss would end their season.

A crowd of more than 24,000 packed Canberra's home ground, and didn't go home disappointed.

Mal Meninga was unstoppable, scoring two tries and finishing the match with a personal haul of eighteen points. Gary Belcher also crossed for a double as the Raiders ran in seven tries in a 40-6 victory.

Canberra finished fourth on the ladder, and played Wests in the minor preliminary semi-final. The Magpies beat Canterbury in a playoff for fifth spot during the week, and came out firing.

Andrew Farrar scored an early try for Wests but Canberra hit back with tries to Gary Belcher and Mal Meninga to take a 12-6 lead to the halftime break.

Mark Bell scored shortly after the resumption of play, and when Belcher crossed for his second, Canberra were home 22-8.

The minor semi-final saw Canberra face Manly. The Sea Eagles went into the match without injured stars Des Hasler, Tony Iro, Michael O'Connor and Ian Roberts; and lost Martin Bella and Geoff Toovey during the game.

Canberra were at their attacking best, and led 28-14 early in the second half before Manly stormed back into the game to make it 28-26 going into the final minutes. Raiders second row forward Gary Coyne crossed for his fourth try to wrap up a 34-26 win for his team. It was the first time a forward had scored four tries in a finals match since Les Cowie for Souths in their 36-33 loss to Balmain in the final of 1956.

Canberra clashed with North Sydney in the final for a place in the premiership decider against Penrith. Norths were considered unlucky to gown 16-14 to Penrith in their semi-final, despite scoring three tries to two.

Tries to solid fullback Paul Conlon and utility John McArthur gave Norths an early 12-0 lead. Canberra hit back to lead 16-14 at halftime, and a hat trick to Paul Martin set up a 30-14 victory.

Canberra advanced to their third consecutive Grand Final, and faced Penrith in a replay of the 1990 decider.

Penrith's veteran hooker Royce Simmons was an unlikely first try scorer in the opening minutes; but Matthew Wood crossed for Canberra to level the scores.

Wood crossed for his second try to give Canberra a 12-6 halftime lead. When Panthers' firebrand second row forward Mark Geyer was sin binned shortly after the break, the Raiders looked set to capitalise.

Geyer returned to the field to set up a try for Brad Izzard which levelled the scores at 12-12. Greg Alexander put Penrith in front with a field goal before Geyer delivered a pass for Simmons to score his second try to wrap up the game 19-12. Penrith had won their first premiership. Despite playing in the losing side, Brad Clyde was awarded the Clive Churchill Medal.

Mal Meninga was the club's top point scorer with 166. He finished one behind winger Paul Martin as the team's top try scorer. Martin finished the year with fourteen tries.

1992

Canberra faced an uncertain future as revelations emerged that they had breached the salary cap during the 1991 season. After the infringement was found, Canberra were forced to offload some of their talent before the 1992 season. Young second row forwards Nigel Gaffey and David Barnhill joined Easts and St George respectively. Mark Bell joined Wests and became one of the top try scorers in the competition. Winger Paul Martin moved to the Gold Coast. Perhaps most importantly, prop forward Glenn Lazarus left the club to play for Brisbane.

Canberra had a new goal kicking forward in David Furner, the son of inaugural coach Don. Steve Stone was an important player in the halves during the season, and New Zealand winger Sean Hoppe became a regular first grader.

Canberra signed St George prop forward Paul Osborne and journeyman utility back Phil Blake from North Sydney. Chris O'Sullivan returned to the club towards the end of the season, and exciting winger Ken Nagas made his first grade debut.

In the opening round of the 1992 season, Canberra faced Penrith in a replay of the last two Grand Finals. The goal kicking of Mal Meninga proved the difference as the Raider ran out winners 14-10 at Bruce Stadium.

The Raiders were beaten 28-16 by Manly at Brookvale in round two; and lost 24-16 to Brisbane at home the following week.

The problems for Canberra were highlighted in their round four loss to Illawarra. The Steelers scored five tries to two in a 29-10 win which left Canberra with just one win from their opening four games.

Canberra finally found their best form in round five, scoring seven tries in a 40-16 win over Cronulla. Rookie centre David Boyle scored two tries, and Mal Meninga, playing second row, finished the game with fourteen points.

The Raiders lost to 12-10 to a Wally Lewis captained Gold Coast the following week, before beating Newcastle 26-20 at Brice Stadium. Despite their inconsistency, the Raiders remained just a win short of the top five.

Canberra went down 27-18 to North Sydney in round eight, and fell further behind the leaders when they were beaten 34-20 by Balmain at Leichhardt Oval in round nine.

In round ten rookie forward David Furner scored three tries and scored 22 points as Canberra beat Parramatta 31-12.

Canberra lost 24-8 to Easts at the Sydney Football Stadium in round eleven, and turned the halfway mark of the competition in equal tenth place with Manly; five points adrift of the top five.

Rookie winger Jason Croker scored two of Canberra's five tries in their round twelve 27-18 win over Wests at Bruce Stadium.

A 16-10 home win over St George the following week saw the Raiders within three points of the top five; and they inched even closer after beating Souths 24-22 at the Sydney Football Stadium.

Canberra made it four in a row in round fifteen; beating Canterbury 39-14 at Bruce Stadium. The home side ran in seven tries including a double to the evergreen Phil Blake.

The Raiders' momentum stalled when they were edged out 10-8 by Penrith; and 15-14 by Manly. The losses proved costly, with Canberra in ninth place; five points outside of the top five with just five rounds to play.

In round eighteen Canberra were comfortable beaten 28-12 by the competition leading Brisbane Broncos at Lang Park. Young winger Willie Carne scored a double for the home side.

Canberra kept their finals chances alive when they demolished Illawarra 38-2 at home. Bill Mullins scored a double, and second row forward David Furner kicked seven goals from as many attempts.

The next week Canberra travelled to Sydney to play Cronulla, who had no chance of making the finals. The Raiders put in a lacklustre performance, and their chances of making the playoffs disappeared in a 22-4 loss.

Canberra produced a strong effort in their last home match of the season, beating Gold Coast by 33-10. However, their season was typified by inconsistency, and they lost their last match, to Newcastle 22-11.

Canberra finished in the unfamiliar position of twelfth on the ladder. It was the first time they had missed the finals since 1986.

Although the salary cap issues, and injuries at key times contributed; the roster was strong enough to challenge for a spot in the finals for much of the season.

David Furner was the club's point scorer with 102, and looked to be a star of the future. As did fullback Brett Mullins, who was the club's leading try scorer with eleven.

1993

The depth in Canberra's halves took a hit before the start of the 1993 season. Veterans Chris O'Sullivan, Craig Bellamy and Scott Gale retired; while Phil Blake left after just one season to continue his career at St George. The Raiders still had Ricky Stuart and Laurie Daley, but lacked experienced backup in case of injury.

Canberra looked overseas to bolster their ranks, as they continued to balance their salary cap. New Zealand forwards John Lomax and Quentin Pongia joined the club, as did Fijian winger Noa Nadruku who became one of the sensations of the season. Another Kiwi, centre Ruben Wiki made his first grade debut during the season.

Apart from Stuart and Daley, Canberra still had Gary Belcher, Mal Meninga, Jason Croker, Brett Mullins and Sean Hoppe in their backline, and a forward pack that included Brad Clyde, David Furner, Steve Walters and Paul Osborne. There was considerable hope that the 1992 season was just an aberration.

The 1993 season did not begin well for the Raiders. They faced runners up St George in round one at Bruce Stadium, and were outclassed 22-8.

A three tries to one 18-8 win over Penrith in the second round gave fans cause for cautious optimism; as did the following week's 17-10 win over Balmain at Leichhardt, which saw the Raiders sit just one point outside of the top five.

In round four, Canberra ventured to Brisbane to play the 1992 premiers. A crowd of 46,000 fans watched an intense match which ended in a 12-10 win for the home side.

Canberra found their best form the following week, running in nine tries in a 46-6 mauling of Cronulla. Wingers Sean Hoppe and Noa Nadruku both crossed for doubles.

A narrow 10-8 loss to Parramatta followed, and Canberra looked again like being plagued by inconsistency.

The Raiders scored six tries to two in a 27-10 home win over high fliers Canterbury in round seven, before sneaking home 15-10 against Easts in Perth. They made it three in a row for the first time in round nine, crushing Gold Coast 48-4. Sean Hoppe scored a hat trick, and Ricky Stuart and Noa Nadruku crossed for doubles in the win which saw the Raiders in the top five for the first time all season.

More than 17,000 people attended Brookvale Oval for the round ten clash between Manly and Canberra. The Raiders continued to gain momentum with a 21-10 victory.

Noa Nadruku scored a hat trick and David Furner contributed sixteen points as Canberra smashed Souths 41-10 at Bruce Stadium in round eleven. At the halfway mark of the competition the Raiders were in equal fourth spot with Brisbane; two points behind competition leaders Canterbury and St

George, and just a point adrift of third placed North Sydney.

In round twelve Canberra suffered a 28-14 upset loss at Newcastle, but bounced back with a straight forward 38-16 win over Illawarra the following week to stay in fourth spot.

A crowd of 22,000 packed North Sydney Oval in round fourteen to watch the home side take on the Raiders. Noa Nadruku scored two tries to help Canberra to a 24-20 victory; although the Bears stayed a point ahead in third spot.

Nadruku was proving a try scoring sensation for the Raiders, and crossed for another hat trick in their round fifteen 38-2 thumping of Wests.

The following week, Canberra went to Adelaide to play top of the table St George. Sean Hoppe and Steve Walters both scored twice as Canberra ran out surprisingly easy winners by 30-2. The Raiders moved up to third place, just one win behind St George, who were joined at the top by Canterbury.

After a tough 16-10 win over Penrith; Canberra fell back to fourth place when their home match against Balmain ended in a 32-32 draw.

Canberra re-established their premiership credentials in round nineteen by beating Brisbane 20-4; scoring four tries to one against the premiers.

The Raiders moved into second spot, a point behind Canterbury, after thumping Cronulla 42-12 in round twenty. Jason Croker, now playing lock, scored four tries in the win.

The second last round of the season saw tragedy and triumph for Canberra. They had the biggest win their history; annihilating Parramatta 68-0 at Bruce Stadium to move to the top of the table. However, halfback Ricky Stuart suffered a season ending ankle injury during the match.

The lack of depth in the halves was highlighted in the last round of the season when Canberra went down 32-8 to Canterbury to surrender the minor premiership.

The Raiders dropped to third spot, and prepared for a semi-final match against St George. Canberra moved Laurie Daley to halfback, and Mal Meninga to five-eighth in an attempt to cover the absence of Stuart. The moved looked set to be unsuccessful when tries to Ricky Walford and Mark Coyne set up a 15-0 halftime lead for the Dragons.

Phil Blake, who would have proved a useful substitute for Stuart, scored two second half tries against his former club to give St George an unassailable 25-0 lead.

Meninga and Furner crossed for Canberra towards the end of the match; as did fullback Mick Potter for St George, to give the Dragons a 31-10 victory.

The following week Canberra faced Brisbane in an elimination semi-final. Meninga and Daley moved back to their familiar positions, and Steve Stone was picked at halfback.

Desperate to defend their title, Brisbane were unstoppable in the first half; running in four tries to race to a 24-0 lead. Noa Nadruku scored shortly before the break, but the premiers led 24-4.

Nadruku scored two more tries in the second half to give Canberra some hope; bringing the scoreline to 24-12.

However, former Raider Kevin Walters crossed in the dying minutes to give Brisbane the win by 30-12; ending Canberra's season. Brisbane went on to beat St George in the Grand Final for the second year in a row.

Noa Nadruku was the club's and the competition's leading try scorer with 22 in a sensational rookie season. David Furner topped the point scoring for the Raiders with 162.

Fullback Gary Belcher retired at the end of the 1993 season after close to 150 first grade matches for the Raiders. He also scored more than 500 points, and won two premierships.

1994

Canberra were quiet in the player transfer market during the off-season. The loss of Gary Belcher allowed Brett Mullins to make the fullback position his own; and culminated in selection for Australia. Winger Sean Hoppe left the club to join North Sydney. Ken Nagas would prove successful in securing a position on the wing in his absence.

John Lomax and Quentin Pongia became permanent fixtures in the forward pack, as did Brett Hetherington and David Westley. Local hooker Simon Woolford made his first grade debut during the season.

Ricky Stuart made a successful return from injury and joined regulars David Furner, Jason Croker, Laurie Daley, Brett Mullins, Noa Nadruku, Steve Walters and Brad Clyde in a formidable line up. They key player remained captain of club, state and country; the veteran Mal Meninga.

Canberra again struggled in the opening round of the season, going down 24-16 to Cronulla at Endeavour Field.

They bounced back in round two; smashing Souths 46-16 at home. Brad Clyde scored a double as the Raiders ran in nine tries.

Canberra moved into the top five with a 34-8 home win over Newcastle in round three. Centre Ruben Wiki crossed for four tries, while Jason Croker, playing winger, scored twice.

In round four, Canberra faced 1993 minor premiers Canterbury at Belmore. The Bulldogs proved too strong, winning 17-12 to knock the Raiders out of the top five.

Canberra snuck back into fifth place the following week by beating Illawarra 30-16 on the back of two tries from Brett Mullins. They consolidated their place in the top five with a 40-24 win over Wests at Campbelltown. Croker, at five-eighth scored a hat trick.

The Raiders were back at home in round seven to face a Manly side bolstered by the acquisitions of Mark Carroll, Terry Hill and David Gillespie. The Sea Eagles proved no match for the home side; going down 30-6.

Canberra easily accounted for Parramatta 24-10 before suffering a shock 8-4 loss to last placed Gold Coast in round nine.

They took their frustration out on St George at home the following week; thumping the Dragons 40-10.

A 38-4 win over Easts, built on hat tricks to Jason Croker and Jason Death, saw the Raiders turn the midway point of the season in second spot; four points behind Canterbury.

Canberra dropped to fourth place in round twelve after suffering a shock 30-16 away loss to Penrith. They bounced back to beat the premiers, Brisbane by 29-10, but stayed in fourth spot behind the Bulldogs, Manly and North Sydney.

The Raiders fell further behind the leaders by going down 25-10 to Norths; but stayed in the top five with a 36-0 thumping of Balmain and a ten tries to two 56-12 annihilation of Cronulla. Brett Mullins scored a hat trick for the Raiders in that win, which consolidated fourth place.

In round seventeen, Canberra kept up their scintillating form with a 48-8 win over Souths at the Sydney Football Stadium. Mullins scored four of his side's ten tries.

Mullins made it eleven tries in just three weeks when he crossed for four in Canberra's 52-16 win over Newcastle in round eighteen. The Raiders remained in fourth place with four rounds to play.

More than 20,000 fans attended Bruce Stadium to watch Canberra smash Canterbury 36-6 to lay down the gauntlet to the top teams. Ruben Wiki scored three of their seven tries.

Canberra beat Illawarra 19-8, and Wests 40-22; but remained stuck in fourth spot despite seven wins in a row. They travelled to Brookvale to face Manly in the final round; with the winner guaranteed a top three finish.

A crowd of over 26,000 packed Brookvale confident Manly could go into the finals on a roll, after winning their last five matches. Both sides scored three tries, but a David Furner penalty goal and a Ricky Stuart field goal saw the Raiders come from behind to win 21-18. Canberra leap frogged Manly into third spot, and set up a semi-final clash with North Sydney.

Jason Croker, Noa Nadruku and Ken Nagas scored first half tries to give Canberra a 14-0 halftime lead. When Quentin Pongia crossed shortly after the break, the Raiders went to an unassailable 20-0 lead. Croker scored late in the match to wrap up a 26-12 victory.

Brett Mullins and Mal Meninga scored first half tries for Canberra in their semi-final against Canterbury; but silly penalties allowed the boot of Daryl Halligan to give the Bulldogs a 14-12 lead at halftime.

Canterbury went further ahead before prop forward David Westley crossed in the last minute. David Furner's conversion locked up the match at 18-18, and extra time was required. With just two minutes of extra time to play, Halligan kicked a field goal for Canterbury to advance them into the Grand Final.

Canberra played North Sydney in the final, and when Bears' hooker Mark Soden scored early, the Raiders knew they had a fight on their hands to make the premiership decider.

Midway through the first half prop John Lomax was sent from the field for a high tackle; further diminishing the chances of the Raiders. The ledger was squared though just minutes later when Norths' forwards Gary Larson was also sent off.

Mal Meninga scored for Canberra, but a Jason Taylor field goal kept Norths ahead 7-6 at the half time break.

Meninga was at his best after the break, setting up tries for Noa Nadruku, Ken Nagas and Brett Mullins to give Canberra a 24-9 victory.

Canberra went into the 1994 Grand Final against Canterbury knowing it would be the last game for the club for inspirational leader Mal Meninga.

The hero of the first half was prop Paul Osborne, who was picked in the side to replace the suspended John Lomax. He produced two magic offloads to set up tries for David Furner and Ken Nagas in the opening stages of the first half.

When Laurie Daley scored, Canberra led 14-0. Canterbury winger crossed from an intercept before Noa Nadruku scored to give Canberra a well-deserved 18-6 halftime lead.

Ken Nagas scored a second try shortly after the break, and when Jason Croker crossed Canberra had a 30-6 lead midway through the second half.

Canterbury hooker Jason Hetherington scored a try to narrow the gap; but in the final minutes, Mal

Meninga received the send-off he deserved when he intercepted a pass to score a try and converted to give Canberra an emphatic 36-12 victory. David Furner was awarded the Clive Churchill Medal.

Mal Meninga finished his career captaining the 1994 Kangaroos squad on the tour of Great Britain and France. He was joined by teammates David Furner, Laurie Daley, Brad Clyde, Steve Walters, Ricky Stuart and Brett Mullins.

Although Meninga retired at the end of the tour, the future looked bright for Canberra. However, the introduction of pay television, and the vacancy of the Australian captaincy saw Canberra as a key prize in what would become known as the Super League war.

During the 1994 season, the Australian Rugby League hierarchy, led by Ken Arthurson and John Quayle, announced four new teams would join the competition in 1995. A second team in Brisbane, known as the South Queensland Crushers, provided enough of a catalyst for the Brisbane Broncos to be aggrieved.

Teams from North Queensland, based in Townsville; Auckland, and Perth gained inclusion into the expanded competition; but a much bigger picture was unfolding as the owners of new pay television operators Optus Vision and Foxtel battled with traditional broadcaster Channel Nine. The brawl would cast a dark shadow over the 1995 season.

1995

Canberra went into the 1995 season without Mal Meninga for the first time in a decade. The Queensland and Australian captain retired after becoming the first player to lead a Kangaroo Tour for a second time.

The Raiders retained the rest of their premiership winning side except for prop Paul Osborne who announced his retirement.

Shortly before the expanded competition began, representatives from a number of clubs, including Canberra, had met with executives from News Limited to discuss the formation of a twelve team Super League.

As far as the public knew, it was business as usual as the Raiders began their premiership defence against the new South Queensland Crushers side in Brisbane. Jason Croker scored two of Canberra's five tries in their 24-6 victory.

In round two, Canberra returned to Bruce Stadium to face Penrith. David Furner kicked seven goals, and Brett Mullins crossed for two tries in a comfortable 34-12 win.

Brad Clyde scored a double for the Raiders in their round three 34-18 win over Parramatta; and they retained a share of the competition lead by beating North Queensland 14-8 the following week.

On the same day as their round four win, Canberra were one of three clubs requested to show cause why they should not be excluded from the competition, following revelations they had agreed to play in the proposed Super League competition. The Australian Rugby League also made the decision to exclude any Super League aligned players from representative selection during the 1995 season.

Back on the field, Canberra remained undefeated after beating St George 17-4 at home in round five. The following week they beat Canterbury (playing as the Sydney Bulldogs) 16-6 at Belmore.

Canberra beat the Perth based Western Reds by 28-21 in round seven to retain a four way share of the competition lead alongside Manly, Brisbane and Newcastle.

More than 23,000 fans attended Bruce Stadium in round eight to watch the match of the day between Canberra and Brisbane. In what was expected to be a close tussle, the Raiders scored five tries in a 26-0 victory.

Canberra beat Norths 20-18 in round nine to set up a top of the table clash with Manly at Bruce Stadium.

Both clubs were the flagships of the opposite sides of the rugby league civil war. By the time of their round ten clash, the public were well aware of the schism within the game; and tensions were running high.

In a classic struggle, Canberra led for most of the match before Manly winger John Hopoate scored his third try to wrap up a 16-8 victory for the Sea Eagles. It was Canberra's first loss of the season.

Canberra bounced back to beat Illawarra 16-8, before running in ten tries on their way to a 50-12 thumping of Parramatta. Off the field, the fight for rugby league spilled into the courts, with a decision to be made towards the end of the season.

The Raiders snuck home 17-16 against Easts, who were now playing under the banner of the Sydney Roosters. The win kept Canberra in equal second place with Newcastle.

Canberra and the Knights faced off at Bruce Stadium in round fourteen. Jason Croker scored two tries, and David Furner amassed eighteen points as Canberra ran out winners 39-4.

The following week, Canberra suffered a shock 38-12 loss to Cronulla at Endeavour Field, and were again caught by Newcastle in equal second spot.

Young backs Albert Fulivai and Michael Maguire both scored doubles for Canberra in their 28-10 win over Balmain in round sixteen. Manly lost for the first time all season; and the Raiders moved to within a win of the competition lead.

Albert Fulivai crossed twice in Canberra's 24-12 win over Penrith, before Jason Croker scored a hat trick as the Raiders thrashed Wests 50-18. With four rounds to play, Canberra had joined Manly at the top of the table.

Brett Mullins, Jason Croker and Noa Nadruku all scored doubles for Canberra as they thumped Souths 46-12 in round nineteen.

The Raiders continued their attacking rampage against Gold Coast. They scored ten tries in a 56-6 annihilation, with Nadruku scoring a hat trick, and Laurie Daley, Ken Nagas and Ruben Wiki all notching doubles.

Canberra beat Auckland 15-8 in the second last round, and finished the regular season with seven wins in a row after smashing South Queensland by 58-4. Ken Nagas scored four tries in the win.

The Raiders finished equal first with Manly, but missed out on the minor premiership on percentages. In the newly expanded eight team finals format, Canberra played third placed Brisbane in their quarter final.

The sides met at Lang Park in Brisbane in the first ever finals match played outside of Sydney. Steve Walters scored Canberra's lone try in the first half, and a field goal from Ricky Stuart gave them a 7-6 lead at the break. Brad Clyde scored the only try of the second half, and Canberra ran out winners by 14-8.

Canberra earned a week off with the win, and next played Canterbury for a spot in the Grand Final. The Bulldogs had endured a season of turmoil when four of their Super League aligned players changed their mind, and sided with the ARL. It was a tribute to coach Chris Anderson that the club was still a premiership threat.

Canberra couldn't find their rhythm in the first half and went to the break behind 11-0. Brett Mullins scored shortly after the break to make it 11-6, but

Terry Lamb dominated for the Bulldogs, setting up a 25-6 win. They defeated Manly in the Grand Final the following week.

It was a disappointing end to Canberra's premiership defence. They had lost just two matches during the regular season, and had the misfortunate to run into a more determined Bulldogs side at the wrong end of the season.

David Furner was the club's top point scorer with 198; finishing third in the competition behind Matthew Ridge and Daryl Halligan. Jason Croker was Canberra's top try scorer with fifteen; one ahead of Brett Mullins and Ken Nagas.

The day after the Grand Final, the Australian Rugby League began their court case to prevent the Super League competition was beginning. Shortly before the kick off of the 1996 season, the court found in favour of the ARL. The Super League aligned clubs, including Canberra, faced the distinct possibility of sitting out the 1996 season.

1996

Canberra retained their 1995 squad, and added rugby convert Ben Kennedy. Rookie utility back Luke Phillips made his first grade debut during the season, as did young front rower Todd Payten.

With the court finding in favour of the Australian Rugby League, the first round of the 1996 season descended into chaos when the teams aligned with Super League refused to play. Canberra forfeited their first round match against South Queensland.

Common sense prevailed, and the competition resumed as normal. Canberra and Penrith played out a 12-12 draw; and the Raiders went down to Parramatta in round three by 20-14.

Canberra won for the first time in 1996 in spectacular fashion. Their round four match against North Queensland ended in a 66-10 victory, with Ruben Wiki scoring four of the Raiders' twelve tries.

The Raiders came back to earth the following week when they were beaten 30-20 by St George at Kogarah in front of almost 17,000 people.

In round six, Canberra faced an equally struggling Canterbury at Bruce Stadium. The Raiders proved too strong, winning 34-4, with wingers Ken Nagas and Noa Nadruku both scoring two tries.

Jason Croker scored two of Canberra's six tries in their 32-12 win over Western Reds in Perth; but were smashed 50-16 by Brisbane in round eight.

Canberra seemed happier in front of their home crowd in 1996; and in round nine they crushed second placed North Sydney 46-12, with David Furner finishing the match with eighteen points.

The Raiders' inconsistent season continued with a 28-12 loss to manly at Brookvale Oval, followed by a 16-14 win over Illawarra. At the halfway mark of the competition, Canberra sat in tenth spot; a point short of the top eight.

Canberra suffered a humiliating 50-10 loss to Parramatta in round twelve. The Raiders conceded nine tries to a side just one place ahead of them on the ladder.

The Raiders hit back with a 16-12 win over Sydney Roosters and a 16-14 victory at Newcastle to again be within a point of the top eight. They lost 24-16 to Cronulla to again stall their momentum.

In round sixteen, Canberra beat Balmain 28-10; and finally broke into the top eight with a 32-16 home win over Penrith the following week.

A 24-16 loss to Wests in round eighteen saw the Raiders fall back out of the top eight as the competition tightened with four rounds to play.

Canberra snuck back into the eight with a 40-10 win over Souths on the back of two tries from makeshift fullback Ken Nagas. The Raiders won without Brett Mullins, Jason Croker and Ricky Stuart.

A 26-12 win over Gold Coast consolidated Canberra's place in the top eight; and they wrapped up a spot in the finals when Ken Nagas notched a hat trick in their 30-6 win over Auckland in the second last round.

In the final round Noa Nadruku scored four of Canberra's seven tries in their 36-10 win over South Queensland in Brisbane. The Raiders finished the season in sixth spot. Canberra's season came to an end the following week when they were run down 16-14 by St George in an elimination semi-final.

David Furner was the club's top point scorer with 144, while Noa Nadruku topped the competition's try scoring list with 22.

1997

In October 1996, the Super League competition was given the green light after winning a court appeal. Canberra were one of eight teams that left the Australian Rugby League to participate in the breakaway league. They were joined by a new team from Adelaide, and a team based in Newcastle, known as the Hunter Mariners.

Canberra welcomed Mal Meninga back to the club in 1997. He was appointed head coach, replacing Tim Sheens who moved to North Queensland.

Veteran hooker Steve Walters joined Sheens at the Cowboys after more than 220 games and a decade at the Raiders. New Zealand test prop John Lomax also followed Sheens.

Young hooker Luke Priddis challenged Simon Woolford to see who replace Walters; but the rest of the squad remained intact.

In the first round of the new league, Canberra were comprehensive beaten 26-4 by Cronulla. The following week they went down 33-20 to Penrith to find themselves in the uncustomary position of last place on the ladder.

In round three, seven goals from Daryl Halligan helped Canterbury to a 38-26 home win over the Raiders. Brisbane kept Canberra winless after four rounds with a 24-8 victory in Brisbane.

The Raiders finally broke through for their first win of the season in round five, beating Hunter Mariners 18-12.

A 31-24 loss to Auckland left the Raiders in last place, but they started their comeback with a 30-20 win over Penrith on the back of three tries from Ben Kennedy.

Brett Mullins scored two of Canberra's seven tries in their 40-16 win over North Queensland. A 30-10 win over Perth saw the Raiders move into the top five for the first time all season as the competition reached its midway point.

Two tries from Brett Mullins helped Canberra to a 22-8 win over Cronulla in round ten which kept the Raiders in fifth place. A 20-10 win over Auckland saw them move up to fourth spot.

The Raiders moved up to third place with a six tries to three 34-18 win over Adelaide; but they suffered a shock 16-12 loss to Hunter the following week to drop back to fifth spot.

At the end of round fourteen Canberra enjoyed a four way share of second place; five points behind runaway leaders Brisbane. The Raiders defeated Canterbury 28-10 to join Cronulla and Penrith.

Canberra were no match for the Broncos in round fifteen, going down 19-4. They bounced back to beat North Queensland 22-14 to stay in fourth spot.

In round seventeen, Canberra were back to their best, running in ten tries in a 58-16 thrashing of Adelaide. Brett Mullins scored a hat trick, and David Furner finished with a personal haul of twenty points.

A 36-16 away win over Perth saw Canberra in third spot. Ben Kennedy and Noa Nadruku both crossed for doubles in the seven tries to three win.

In the first finals match of the Super League competition, Canberra travelled to Endeavour Field to play Cronulla. Mat Rogers was the star for the Sharks, scoring fourteen points in a 22-18 victory.

The following week Canberra were at home in an elimination semi-final against Penrith. Laurie Daley scored sixteen points in a comprehensive 32-12 win.

Canberra's season came to an end with a 10-4 loss to Cronulla in the preliminary final. Mat Rogers scored all ten of Cronulla's points as they advanced to the Grand Final, which they lost to Brisbane.

David Furner was again Canberra's top point scorer for the season with 116. Exciting forward Ben Kennedy was their leading try scorer with fifteen.

At the end of the season, the Australian Rugby League reached out to News Limited in an effort to end the split in the game. An agreement was achieved, and the National Rugby League was born.

The agreement included a goal of reducing the number of teams in the competition to fourteen by 2000. Canberra were safe from rationalisation, and entered the 1998 season without the axe over their head that plagued several Sydney teams for the next two years.

1998

Canberra entered the National Rugby League with the bulk of their Super League squad. Try scoring winger Noa Nadruku left the club to reunite with former coach Tim Sheens at North Queensland; while forward Quentin Pongia returned to New Zealand. The Raiders had an exciting new utility back in Mark McLinden, while centre Brandon Pearson became a regular first grader.

Canberra drew Canterbury at Belmore in the opening round, and went down 20-10. With Brett Mullins and Ken Nagas unavailable, Laurie Daley played fullback for the Raiders.

In round two, winger David Boyle scored a hat trick for Canberra, but it wasn't enough to prevent the Raiders going down 28-24 to Penrith.

Canberra broke through for their first win of the season in round three, beating Gold Coast 18-4. The following week they went down 14-12 to North Queensland.

Jason Croker scored two of Canberra's five tries in a 26-20 win over a struggling Manly at Bruce Stadium in round five. They went down 22-20 to Illawarra before having another win over Gold Coast 24-12.

In round eight, Canberra had a solid 22-12 win over Balmain. The following week they entered the expanded top ten with a 24-18 win over Adelaide.

David Boyle scored another hat trick in round ten as Canberra thumped North Queensland 50-12. Mark McLinden and Ben Kennedy both crossed for doubles as the Raiders ran in nine tries.

Canberra went down 25-18 to Auckland, but a hard fought 24-18 win over Brisbane in round twelve saw the Raiders turned the halfway mark of the season in eighth spot. Just four points separated fifth place from twelfth.

The Raiders scored five tries to two in a 24-12 win over Manly at Brookvale Oval; but again failed to capitalise on the momentum by going down 34-22 to North Sydney. They beat Newcastle 22-12, but had their premiership credentials called into question when they were thumped 40-12 by the Sydney Roosters.

The inconsistencies continued with a 16-12 win over Cronulla followed by a 24-22 loss to Canterbury. In round nineteen David Boyle scored his third hat trick of the season as Canberra scored nine tries in a 46-16 blitzing of South Sydney.

Canberra then beat Parramatta 22-8, and ran in eight tries on their way to a 48-26 thumping of Penrith. With three rounds to play, Canberra had wrapped up a finals spot, settling in seventh spot.

The Raiders were much too strong for Wests, winning 22-0, and then defeated St George 28-24 at Bruce Stadium. In the last round of the season, Canberra went down 16-12 to Melbourne to finish seventh.

The expanded finals format saw Canberra clash with tenth placed Manly in an elimination final. After Terry Hill scored an early try for the Sea Eagles, Canberra hit back with tries to Brandon Pearson and Brett Mullins and led 10-4 at halftime. A try to replacement forward Todd Payten wrapped up a 17-4 victory.

Canberra advanced to a minor semi-final against the new Melbourne Storm franchise. The Storm were much too strong, scoring five tries to two in a 24-10 win to end Canberra's season.

David Furner scored 168 points to once again be Canberra's top scorer. Rookie back Mark McLinden was the top try scorer for the Raiders with twelve, one ahead of David Boyle.

1999

In major off-season player transfer news, Canberra stalwarts Ricky Stuart and Brad Clyde left the club at the end of 1998 to join Canterbury. Both players had won Clive Churchill Medals in premiership wins. Stuart had played more than 200 first grade games for the Raiders, while Clyde had notched up close to 180.

Canberra had cause for confidence as their side still included Laurie Daley, Brett Mullins, Ken Nagas, David Furner, Ben Kennedy, Jason Croker, Ruben Wiki and Simon Woolford.

Rookies Brandon Pearson and Mark McLinden had become regular first graders after impressive debut seasons, while Todd Payten continued to improve. Young utility forward Luke Williamson and halfback Brett Finch made their first grade debuts for the club during the season.

Gold Coast and Adelaide were removed from the premiership at the end of 1998, while St George merged with Illawarra to form a seventeen team competition.

Canberra drew 1998 premiers Brisbane in round one. 20,000 fans attended Bruce Stadium to watch their team upset the Broncos 28-20.

South Sydney were the surprise packet early in the season, and beat Canberra 21-14 at the Sydney Football Stadium in round two.

Canberra went down 16-14 to the newly merged St George-Illawarra side in round three; but bounced back when Brett Mullins and Laurie Daley both scored twice in the Raiders' 38-14 win over Wests.

Canberra had the bye in round five, and were well refreshed in time to thrash Manly 36-6 in round six. The win saw the Raiders move up to sixth place.

The Raiders fell out of the top eight the following week when they were annihilated 44-2 by St George-Illawarra at Kogarah. A 21-21 draw with Newcastle followed, before the unpredictable Canberra thrashed Norths 37-8.

Inconsistent results again followed; with an 18-14 loss to Canterbury; a 32-30 loss to Auckland; and a 25-12 win over Parramatta. After going down by 28-22 to Sydney Roosters in round thirteen; Canberra were in tenth spot at the midway point of the season.

In round fourteen Canberra scored four tries to one to upset Melbourne 26-6 at Bruce Stadium. The following week Brett Mullins scored two tries as Canberra beat Manly 29-16, which left the Raiders one point short of the top eight.

Parramatta beat Canberra 12-4 at Bruce Stadium in round sixteen; but the Raiders defeated Canterbury 18-2 in Sydney to stay close to the top eight.

In round eighteen Canberra scored eight tries to four in a 46-22 win over Auckland. They were then defeated 24-8 to Cronulla and 30-10 to Melbourne to place their finals chances in jeopardy.

Brett Mullins scored another double for Canberra as they defeated North Queensland 30-8 at Bruce Stadium in round 21.

The Raiders were at their devastating best the following week when they ran in twelve tries on their way to a 64-16 thumping of Wests at Campbelltown. Young halfback Andrew McFadden scored a hat trick, while Luke Williamson, playing centre, kicked eight goals.

In round 23, Canberra were again at their attacking best. Jason Croker scored four of their nine tries in a 46-16 win over Norths. The win left Canberra still a win short of the top eight.

Canberra had the bye in round 24, but a 33-14 loss to Penrith saw the Raiders relying on results to go their way in the final round in order to qualify for the finals.

In the final round of the season, Canberra smashed Balmain 42-14 at Bruce Stadium. Winger Lesley Vainikolo scored three tries, as did Luke Williamson, who finished the match with twenty points.

The win was not enough to clinch a place in the top eight. Canberra fell a point short of eighth placed Brisbane to miss the finals for the first time since 1992.

Luke Williamson capped a successful first season with the Raiders by finishing as the club's top scorer with 174. Jason Croker was the club's top try scorer with fourteen.

Rugby league was again thrown into turmoil at the end of the 1999 season, as traditional Sydney clubs lost their identities. Wests and Balmain merged to form the Wests Tigers; while Manly and Norths had an uneasy marriage to form the ill-fated Northern Eagles franchise.

The greatest uproar was reserved for the exclusion of South Sydney in the new fourteen competition for 2000. Protests in the streets of Sydney ensued, and rugby league again found itself in the courts in the early years of the new millennium.

2000

Canberra went into the 2000 season with much the same squad that narrowly missed the 1999 finals. Young forward Alan Tongue became a regular first grader during the season, and would go on to become a club stalwart. He replaced Ben Kennedy who moved to Newcastle.

Simon Woolford and David Furner were try scorers for the Raiders in their 14-2 win over Canterbury at Bruce Stadium in the opening round of the season.

The Raiders scored four tries to two in a 22-8 win over Northern Eagles to claim a three way share of the competition lead.

Canberra looked back to being a genuine premiership threat by beating 1999 premiers Melbourne 16-12 in round three, to become outright premiership leaders.

Canberra suffered their first loss of the season in round four; going down 18-10 to the new Wests Tigers franchise at Leichhardt Oval.

The Raiders were unstoppable in their next match against Auckland. They scored eleven tries, including doubles to Brett Mullins, Laurie Daley and Lesley Vainikolo on their way to a 56-12 victory.

Fears that inconsistency would again plague Canberra's season surfaced the following week when they were crushed 40-10 by Newcastle. A 14-6 loss to Brisbane in round seven saw them drop down to fifth place.

Canberra had a resounding 30-6 home win over Penrith; but lost 24-18 to St George-Illawarra at the Sydney Football Stadium to fall five points behind competition leaders Brisbane.

In round ten, Canberra had a hard fought 24-18 victory over Cronulla to keep their spot at third on the ladder. They were joined by the Sharks and Sydney Roosters the next week when they fell 14-2 to Parramatta.

Canberra then lost 21-14 to the Roosters, and by 18-16 to the Northern Eagles to turn the midway point of the season in the top eight only through percentages.

In a major upset, Canberra beat competition leaders Brisbane 16-14 at Bruce Stadium in round fourteen. The raiders then had a solid 17-10 win over North Queensland to move back up to fourth place on the ladder.

In such a tightly contested competition, every match counted, and Canberra fell back to seventh spot after losing 26-18 to Cronulla.

In round seventeen Canberra beat the second placed Wests Tigers 24-22 at Bruce Stadium. The Raiders stayed in the top eight, while it began the demise of the Tigers.

A tough 13-6 away win over Auckland saw Canberra climb back into third spot; equal with the Tigers, Penrith and Sydney Roosters.

Halfback Andrew McFadden was the star in their 32-24 win over Newcastle which saw the Raiders move into second spot; four points behind Brisbane.

A 16-14 win over Canterbury seemed to exhaust Canberra as they fell 36-14 to Penrith in their next match. With five rounds to play the Raiders were in third spot; but just a win ahead of eighth.

A 30-20 loss to a desperate St George-Illawarra saw Canberra's chances of making the top four take a dent. However the following week they decimated the high flying Sydney Roosters 40-12 on the back of doubles to Brett Mullins and Jason Croker. The win saw Canberra rise back to second spot.

Parramatta cruelled Canberra's momentum in round 24; running in eight tries in a 48-10 mauling of the Raiders. The loss saw Canberra drop from second spot to sixth.

Canberra somehow recovered to beat Melbourne 20-16; and a 28-14 win over North Queensland in the final round saw the raiders finish the season in fourth spot.

Canberra faced Penrith in the qualifying final, and were down 16-6 just before the break. Halfback Brett Finch scored to narrow the gap at halftime.

In the second half, Canberra were unstoppable, with Jason Croker, Todd Payten, Andrew McFadden and Jamaal Lolesi scoring tries to set up a 34-16 victory. Croker, McFadden and hooker Simon Woolford were cited after the match and suspended for the next clash against Sydney Roosters.

An under strength Canberra side proved no match for the Roosters, who ran in six tries in their 38-10 win which ended the Raiders' season. The Roosters went on to the Grand Final, but were beaten by Brisbane.

David Furner was Canberra's top point scorer in 2000 with 88; just one ahead of Luke Williamson. Winger Lesley Vainikolo was the club's top try scorer with thirteen.

Laurie Daley retired at the end of the season after more than 240 first grade matches. Furner and Mullins also left, as the Raiders started a new era.

2001

With Laurie Daley retired, and David Furner and Brett Mullins moving to England to finish their careers; Canberra were entering a true transitional stage. Halves Mark McLinden and Brett Finch were now the key players in the backline which still featured Ken Nagas and Lesley Vainikolo.

The Raiders signed goal kicking fullback Clinton Schifcofske from Parramatta. Within a year he was playing State of Origin for Queensland.

Young outside backs Joel Monaghan and Michael Robertson made their debuts for the club, as did Joel's brother, halfback Michael.

The Canberra forward pack still featured Luke Davico, Jason Croker, Simon Woolford, Ruben Wiki, Todd Payten and Alan Tongue. They lacked depth, but young prop Ryan O'Hara showed much promise.

Canberra opened their campaign with a 24-6 away win over the newly christened New Zealand Warriors. Schifcofske scored sixteen points on debut for his new club.

Former Manly forward Anthony Colella scored a double for Canberra in their second round bout against Canterbury, but it wasn't enough to prevent a 28-18 loss at Bruce Stadium.

Canberra lost 18-12 to Cronulla, and 24-17 to 2000 runners up Sydney Roosters, to be sharing the bottom of the ladder after four rounds.

In round five, Lesley Vainikolo scored two of Canberra's five tries in their 32-22 home win over St George-Illawarra.

The following week, Canberra moved into the top eight for the first time in the season with a 22-6 win over Parramatta.

Canberra fell out of the top eight with a 26-24 loss to Wests Tigers at Campbelltown, despite a hat trick from centre Jamaal Lolesi.

A 22-20 loss to Newcastle followed before a 34-26 win over lowly North Queensland put the Raiders back within grasp of a top eight spot.

Canberra slumped to a 19-12 loss to Penrith; and a 24-16 loss to Northern Eagles, before gaining a valuable competition point with an entertaining 26-26 draw with Brisbane and Bruce Stadium. Brett Finch scored two tries in a result which saw the Raiders a win outside the top eight.

In round thirteen Canberra went down 32-28 to Melbourne in a match which produced ten tries. The Raiders turned the halfway mark of the competition in eleventh spot.

A home 22-10 loss to the Warriors saw Canberra start to lose touch with the top eight. However, the following week they thumped Canterbury 32-0, with Clinton Schifcofske contributing sixteen points.

The Raiders' inconsistent season continued with a 26-12 loss to Cronulla, followed by a 32-22 upset win over Sydney Roosters, with Schifcofske again notching sixteen points.

The round eighteen match against St George-Illawarra proved that Canberra would struggle to qualify for the finals, much less challenge for the premiership. The Dragons ran in eight tries in a 44-12 win which completely outclassed the Raiders.

Defence was again an issue for Canberra the following week, as they conceded nine tries in a 50-22 loss to Parramatta.

Canberra lost 28-22 to Wests Tigers, and then conceded another nine tries in a 54-26 loss to Newcastle. Andrew Johns scored four tries and 34 points for the Knights in a masterful display.

In round 22 halfback Andrew McFadden scored two of Canberra's five tries in their 29-10 win over North Queensland which kept them a mathematical hope of making the finals.

A 26-24 loss to last placed Penrith the following week ended any chance Canberra had of qualifying for the end of season playoffs. They slumped to a 36-22 home loss to Northern Eagles to move closer to the wooden spoon than the finals.

In the second last round of the season, Canberra gave their fans something to cheer for when they demolished premiers Brisbane on their home turf. Unheralded wingers Rod Jensen and Odell Manual both scored twice as the Raiders ran out winners by 40-18.

In the final round, Canberra scored six tries to one in a 32-6 win over Melbourne in front of their home fans at Bruce Stadium. It was a positive end to a tough season. The Raiders finished in eleventh spot.

Fullback Clinton Schifcofske was a revelation, and finished the season as the club's top point scorer with 245. Brett Finch was Canberra's leading try scorer in 2001 with twelve. Mal Meninga stepped down as coach at the end of the season.

2002

Former St George forward Matthew Elliott took over from Mal Meninga as head coach for the 2002 season. Elliott had served as assistant coach at the Raiders under Meninga, and also had success with Bradford in England.

Elliott inherited much the same squad that missed the finals in 2001. Young prop forward Mark Bryant made his first grade debut for the club, as did outside back Phil Graham.

The biggest talking point before the 2002 season started was the reinstatement of South Sydney, after the club won a protracted court battle to win their place in the competition.

In the opening round of the season, Canberra travelled to Melbourne and went down 16-12 to the Storm in a tough encounter.

Canberra faced the new Rabbitohs side in round two, and were beaten 30-22 at Bruce Stadium in a surprise result.

A crowd of more than 37,000 attended Canberra's round three match against Wests Tigers as part of a double header. The Raiders snuck home 15-10 to record their first win of the season.

Round four saw Canberra crash 52-6 to reigning premiers Newcastle. Andrew Johns kicked eight goals in the match, while centre Mark Hughes scored a hat trick.

Canberra pushed Brisbane all the way in round five, but went down 18-16. The following week they were thrashed 36-12 by Northern Eagles in Gosford.

The Raiders slumped to the bottom of the table in round seven when they were monstered 38-0 by Parramatta. They bounced back to beat Cronulla 36-10 on the back of sixteen points from Clinton Schifcofske, but remained well outside of the top eight.

A 21-21 draw with St George-Illawarra followed before Canberra again went down to Souths, 26-20. In round eleven Phil Graham scored a double in their 32-20 win over North Queensland, which kept them a point ahead of the Cowboys and Penrith at the bottom of the table.

Mark McLinden scored a double in a 28-16 win over Northern Eagles, and a round thirteen bye saw Canberra in ninth place at the halfway mark of the season.

Cronulla continued to be Canberra's bogey team, as they beat the Raiders 36-26 in round fourteen. Sharks halfback Brett Kimmorley scored twenty points in the win.

Canberra fell to their lowest point of the season in round fifteen when they were crushed 46-6 by top of the table Canterbury.

The Raiders in front of their home crowd the following week to beat Penrith 24-12; but were then smashed 36-6 by high fliers Sydney Roosters.

Two tries from Mark McLinden set up a 30-24 win over Newcastle, before a 34-18 loss to the Cowboys again interrupted their momentum. Canberra scored seven tries in a 38-20 win over the Warriors in round twenty to be within a win of the top eight.

The Raiders enjoyed a week off with the bye, and were refreshed enough to thump Wests Tigers by 26-6, thanks to a hat trick from Phil Graham.

The competition was thrown into chaos in round 23 when tearaway leaders Canterbury were stripped of their competition points after being found to be in serious breach of the salary cap. It ensured the Bulldogs would finish the season with the wooden spoon, instead of challenging for their first title since 1995.

The decision meant the teams just outside of the top eight now had an extra spot to play for, but Canberra could not capitalise initially; falling 38-12 to Sydney Roosters.

In round 24, Canberra faced Canterbury at Bruce Stadium. The Bulldogs were determined to finish the season on a high note, but the Raiders had much more to play for, and emerged 38-34 winners in a highly entertaining match.

Canberra were smashed 36-2 by Brisbane in the second last round, and went into their last round clash with Melbourne in equal eighth place with the Storm, and St George-Illawarra.

The Dragons wrapped up their finals spot with a big win over Newcastle. The winner of the Canberra and Melbourne bout would claim the last spot in the finals.

Canberra scored five tries to three to run out 25-16 winners at Bruce Stadium to limp into the finals at the expense of the poorly finishing Northern Eagles, and the disqualified Bulldogs. They tried hard in their finals match against the Warriors, but went down 36-20.

Clinton Schifcofske was again the top point scorer with 140. Rookie Phil Graham was the club's leading try scorer with thirteen.

2003

During the off-season, Canberra lost Andrew McFadden to Parramatta, and Todd Payten to Sydney Roosters. They signed hooker Brad Drew and back rower Ian Hindmarsh from Parramatta, and during the season unveiled rookie forwards Ben Cross and Michael Weyman, who would go on to become representative players. Queensland winger Adam Mogg also became a regular first grader for the Raiders.

Canberra opened their campaign by travelling to Townsville to face North Queensland. Phil Graham and Michael Monaghan both scored twice as the Raiders ran out easy winners by 46-14.

In round two Canberra scored three tries to one in a 15-8 win over Wests Tigers at Leichhardt Oval. They stayed at the top of the table with an 18-14 win over St George-Illawarra the following week.

Phil Graham scored two tries and Clinton Schifcofske notched sixteen points as Canberra beat Penrith 40-28 in round four, to remain undefeated.

Canberra stayed at the top of the ladder in round five with a 36-22 win over Parramatta. Schifcofske finished the match with twenty points.

The Raiders had the bye in round six, and continued on their winning ways with a 26-22 win over the Bulldogs at Bruce Stadium.

Mark McLinden scored two of Canberra's six tries in their 34-12 win over South Sydney at the Sydney Football Stadium in round eight.

Canberra suffered their first loss of the season in round nine; going down 30-10 to Melbourne. The Storm scored four tries to two, but seven goals from Matt Orford inflated the scoreline for the home side.

The Raiders lost 26-18 to Penrith the following week, and were joined at the top of the table by Brisbane. They bounced back with an 18-10 win over the Warriors, and went back to outright leaders with a 20-14 win over Cronulla.

Phil Graham scored a hat trick, and Clinton Schifcofske kicked seven goals for Canberra in their 50-14 thumping of Parramatta in round thirteen which saw the club turn the midway point of the season at the top of the table; a win ahead of Brisbane and Penrith.

Brisbane joined Canberra at the top of the table in round fourteen by beating the Raiders 24-20 in the match of the round, despite Joel Monaghan scoring a hat trick.

Canberra lost 26-18 to the Warriors to drop to second spot, before enjoying a bye in round sixteen to refresh for the run home. However, an 18-8 loss to Melbourne saw them drop to third place; a win behind the Broncos and the Panthers.

A field goal from hooker Brad Drew gave Canberra a 19-18 win over St George-Illawarra at Kogarah in round eighteen.

Two tries from Joel Monaghan and Jamaal Lolesi saw Canberra sneak home 28-26 against Wests Tigers, and when they smashed Cronulla 40-12 in round twenty, the Raiders again shared the competition lead.

The key match of round 21 saw Canberra face Sydney Roosters at the Sydney Football Stadium. The Roosters won a tight match 20-16 to join Canberra and Penrith at the top of the table.

Round 22 saw Canberra play Manly, who had reverted to a stand-alone club after the demise of the Northern Eagles. Joel Monaghan scored four of Canberra's nine tries as they smashed the Sea Eagles 51-16 at Brookvale Oval.

The Raiders suffered a shock 34-28 loss to North Queensland; but wrapped up a top four spot with a 24-16 win over Newcastle.

In the second last round Canberra beat Canterbury 21-16 in Sydney; but lost their last round match to the Roosters by 23-16 to finish the season in fourth spot.

In the first finals match of 2003 Canberra faced Melbourne at Bruce Stadium. Joel Monaghan and Jamaal Lolesi scored early tries to give Canberra a 12-0 lead.

Matt Orford scored, and set up two others to give Melbourne a 16-12 lead at the break. Further tries to Marcus Bai, Cameron Smith and Matt Geyer saw the Storm run out winners by 30-18.

Canberra faced the Warriors in an elimination final, and went to a 10-0 lead on the back of a try to Simon Woolford and three goals from Clinton Schifcofske. Both sides traded tries in the second half to be locked at 16-16. Warriors' halfback kicked a field goal in the dying minutes to give his side a 17-16 win; ending Canberra's season.

Schifcofske scored 222 points for the Raiders, while Joel Monaghan was the club's top try scorer with 21. Despite a poor finals campaign, it appeared Canberra were back as a premiership threat.

2004

Canberra went into the 2004 season with the same squad that had a top four finish in 2003; but they had to compete without Phil Graham and Alan Tongue for much of the season, as both players struggled with injury. Young halves Terry Campese and Todd Carney made their first grade debuts during the season.

Canberra opened their campaign with a 21-12 win over St George-Illawarra at Kogarah; but were crushed 34-18 by premiers Penrith in round two.

A Brad Drew field goal saw the Raiders sneak home 19-18 over North Queensland in round three; and fourteen points from Clinton Schifcofske set up a 26-12 win over Parramatta to see the club as one of six in a share of the competition lead.

The Raiders had the bye in round five; but again lost to Cronulla in round six 38-24. Brad Drew, playing at halfback, was again the hero in round seven when his field goal gave Canberra a 19-18 win over Newcastle.

Canberra were comprehensively beaten 28-8 by Sydney Roosters, and lost 34-20 to Brisbane in round nine to slip to eighth spot. When they were defeated 26-12 by Wests Tigers, they dropped out of the top eight for the first time all season.

A 22-18 loss to Melbourne followed before Canberra hit their straps in a match against Manly at Bruce Stadium in round twelve. Joel Monaghan scored a hat trick as Canberra ran in nine tries in a 48-12 victory.

Canberra lost 20-14 to the Warriors in round thirteen, and turned the halfway mark of the season in eleventh spot; one win outside of the top eight.

In round fourteen Canberra broke their bogey by beating Cronulla 26-16 at Bruce Stadium. Two tries from Phil Graham the following week wasn't enough to prevent a 24-20 loss to Canterbury.

Canberra upset Brisbane on their home turf 21-14 and then defeated Wests Tigers 32-24 to move back into the top eight.

The goal kicking of makeshift five-eight Matt Gafa helped Canberra to a 32-28 win over North Queensland; but the Raiders' spot in the top eight was tenuous after they were smashed 42-8 by Penrith in round nineteen.

Matt Gafa scored three tries and twenty points for Canberra in their round twenty match against the Warriors. The match was decided in golden point, when a second field goal from Clinton Schifcofske gave the Raiders a 30-29 victory.

The following week Canberra conceded seven tries in a 36-22 loss to Manly at Brookvale Oval. A 20-14 loss to Newcastle saw them drop out of the top eight with just four rounds to play.

Canberra were trounced 36-18 by Melbourne; and 38-22 by Sydney Roosters to all but end their finals campaign. They had the bye in the second last round, and found themselves in ninth spot.

Canberra faced last placed South Sydney in the final round of the season. Even if they won, they would need other results to go their way to qualify for the finals.

As it turned out, equal eighth placed sides Wests Tigers and Cronulla lost their final matches. Rookie winger Marshall Chalk scored four tries for Canberra as they demolished Souths 62-22 to clinch a spot in the finals.

The Raiders were bundled out of the finals by the Roosters 38-12. Schifcofske was their top point scorer with 125, ahead of Matt Gafa with 108. Joel Monaghan was top try scorer with twelve.

2005

Brad Drew was the major loss for Canberra at the end of the 2004 season. The club signed veteran utility representative player Jason Smith, and Penrith forward Matt Adamson.

Canberra had the first round bye, and opened their season with a 39-14 win over Newcastle in round two. Clinton Schifcofske scored 23 points for the Raiders.

In round three, Canberra defeated Souths 25-18 to join Manly in a share of the competition lead. They stayed at the top of the table after beating St George-Illawarra 42-22 on the back of nine goals from Schifcofske.

Canberra remained undefeated and went to the outright lead of the competition in round with a solid 24-16 win over Sydney Roosters in front of almost 20,000 fans at Bruce Stadium.

The Raiders suffered their first loss of the season in round six; going down 36-14 to Manly at Brookvale Oval. Manly ran in seven tries, exposing Canberra's defence for the first time.

The following week, Canberra let in eight tries as they slumped to a 46-10 home loss to Melbourne. The loss left the Raiders in a share of second spot, but were fifth on percentages.

Canberra bounced back in round eight, beating Newcastle 14-10; and followed up with a 26-18 victory over Penrith. A 32-26 loss to Cronulla saw the Raiders in fourth spot at the end of round ten.

A mid-season slump followed, with a 28-16 loss to Wests Tigers, and a 30-16 loss to Sydney Roosters. Canberra had their second bye in round thirteen, and were in seventh place at the halfway mark of the competition.

After such a strong start to the season, it was surprising to see Canberra fall out of the top eight in round fourteen after a 20-12 loss to Brisbane.

A 28-10 loss to Canterbury followed; but in round sixteen the Raiders snuck home 23-22 over North Queensland thanks to a field goal from Jason Smith.

The Raiders were on the edge of the top eight in round seventeen after beating Penrith 22-14 at Bruce Stadium. Simon Woolford led the way, scoring two tries.

Canberra were smashed 20-0 by Melbourne the following week. In round nineteen, Phil Graham scored two of Canberra's five tries in a 26-18 win over Parramatta to stay in touch with the top eight.

The Raiders went down 24-16 to the Warriors; 24-18 to Brisbane, and 22-14 to Wests Tigers; but stayed within a win of the top eight.

A 29-16 loss to Souths at Bruce Stadium in round 23 all but ended Canberra's chances of making the finals.

A 31-28 loss to North Queensland saw the Raiders slump to thirteenth spot. They were smashed 48-10 by Parramatta in the second last round, and ended the season with a seventh consecutive loss. Canberra were beaten 36-18 by Manly in the last round, and finished in fifteenth spot; just one win ahead of wooden spooners Newcastle. It was Canberra's worst result since their debut season in 1982.

Fullback Clinton Schifcofske was the club's top point scorer with 142; while Phil Graham was the leading try scorer with twelve.

Matthew Elliott retained his position as head coach, but the club struggled to attract quality players after such a poor finish to the season.

Canberra would continue to rely on a group of young players, who gained much from their experience in 2005. The core of their first grade squad improved the club's position the following year.

2006

Despite not being able to attract players to the club in 2006, Canberra unveiled some exciting new players during the season. Forwards Tom Learoyd-Lahrs and Michael Hodgson became regular first graders, while utility back Lincoln Withers also established his spot. Young fullback William Zillman made his first grade debut for the club.

Canberra started the season with a 27-14 win over Manly at Brookvale Oval. The Raiders scored four tries to three, but five goals from Clinton Schifcofske inflated the margin of the victory.

In round two against Newcastle, Canberra suffered one of the worst defeats in their history. They ran in six tries, including doubles to Phil Graham and William Zillman; but conceded twelve tries as

Newcastle scored a record 70 points. Andrew Johns scored 30 points as the Knights ran out winners 70-32. It was the first time more than 100 points were scored in a match, and continues to hold the premiership record.

Canberra's defensive credentials were left in tatters after going down 56-20 in round three; letting in another ten tries.

Adam Mogg scored two tries, and Clinton Schifcofske kicked a match winning field goal as Canberra beat Penrith 21-20 in golden point in round four.

The Raiders went down 30-12 to Canterbury in round five; but bounced back to beat the Warriors 18-14. They had they bye in round seven to be on the cusp of the top eight.

A crowd of over 23,000 attended Lang Park to watch Brisbane beat Canberra 30-28 in round eight. Both sides scored five tries in the match.

Winger Adrian Purtell scored two of Canberra's five tries in their round nine 30-10 win over Parramatta, which saw the Raiders move back up to ninth place in a tight competition.

Canberra went down 38-28 to Cronulla the following week to fall back to twelfth place; and a

22-12 loss to Newcastle put them further behind the leaders.

In round twelve, Todd Carney kicked a field goal in golden point extra time to give Canberra a 15-14 win over North Queensland.

The Raiders snuck home 24-22 over Souths; and 28-26 over Canterbury to move into equal eighth spot with the Cowboys.

Canberra lost 22-12 to Melbourne, but had their best win of the season in round sixteen; beating Sydney Roosters 42-10. They scored seven tries, and Clinton Schifcofske finished the match with eighteen points.

An 18-12 loss to Parramatta, followed by a 24-12 loss to Penrith saw Canberra fall back to eleventh spot; but they were still within a win of the top eight.

Canberra snuck home 20-18 against Wests Tigers, before beating St George-Illawarra 31-12 at Bruce Stadium on the back of two tries from Todd Carney.

The Raiders went down 21-8 to Souths; but a six tries to three 30-18 win over Brisbane in round 22 saw Canberra move into the top eight for the first time all season.

Canberra won their third golden point match of the season with a 19-18 win over Wests Tigers at Campbelltown, thanks to a field goal from Todd Carney.

The Raiders had the bye in round 24, which secured their spot in the top eight. They went down 22-18 to Melbourne; and finished the season with a 26-24 win over Cronulla at Endeavour Field. Carney scored two of the Raiders' four tries, which saw the club finish in seventh place.

Canberra faced second placed Canterbury in the qualifying final. Jason Smith set up the opening try for Phil Graham to give Canberra the early lead; but they went to the halftime break behind 12-6.

The Bulldogs powered ahead in the second half, and led 30-6 before Adrian Purtell scored in the dying minutes. Canterbury ran out winners 30-12 to end Canberra's season.

Despite the disappointed end of the season, 2006 saw a vast improvement for Canberra. Todd Carney became a top line player, and benefited greatly from playing alongside Jason Smith in the halves.

Clinton Schifcofske was again Canberra's leading point scorer with 178. Todd Carney and Adam Mogg were the club's top try scorers with twelve;

one ahead of Phil Graham and utility forward Alan Tongue.

Matthew Elliott left Canberra at the end of 2006 to coach Penrith. He was replaced by North Queensland assistant coach, and former Raiders lower grade player Neil Henry for the 2007 season.

2007

The 2007 competition was expanded to sixteen teams with the inclusion of Gold Coast. The season was reduced to 25 rounds, with each team receiving a bye during the representative season.

The Neil Henry era at Canberra started without match winning fullback Clinton Schifcofske, who returned to Queensland in 2007 to play rugby union.

Veteran five-eighth Jason Smith also returned to Queensland to play for the North Queensland Cowboys. Centre Adam Mogg left to play with Catalans in France; while captain and hooker Simon Woolford joined St George-Illawarra. Veteran Jason Croker retired at the end of the 2006 season.

The Raiders were forced to go through a major rebuilding period. Their major signing for 2007 was Brisbane utility forward Neville Costigan. Former Easts and Souths forward Scott Logan joined the club, as did veteran try scoring centre Colin Best.

Youngsters Ryan Hinchcliffe, Josh Miller and Bronx Goodwin found regular first grade places; but the holes left by the veterans would prove difficult to fill. Alan Tongue was appointed captain of the club.

Canberra started life under Neil Henry with a 32-6 thrashing at the hands of Manly at Brookvale Oval. The following week they went down 32-16 to Melbourne.

Manly and the Storm would prove to be the best two sides in the competition, but that was small compensation for the Raiders so early in the season.

Canberra found their best form in round three when William Zillman scored a hat trick as the Raiders raced in eight tries in a 48-18 home win over Newcastle. New halfback Michael Dobson kicked eight goals in the victory.

The Raiders fell back to earth in round four when they were smashed 38-6 by Parramatta. The next week Adrian Purtell and Todd Carney both scored two tries as Canberra beat the winless Sydney Roosters 37-28 at Bruce Stadium.

Canberra were crushed 26-0 by Cronulla before bouncing back to beat Penrith on their home turf by 34-18. The Raiders scored six tries in the win.

In a match that produced thirteen tries, Canberra went down 46-30 to Manly at Bruce Stadium in round eight. Former Raiders winger Michael Robertson scored a hat trick for the Sea Eagles.

Canberra beat Souths 16-10, and then enjoyed their bye week to move to the cusp of the top eight by the end of round ten.

Adrian Purtell scored a hat trick as Canberra defeated St George-Illawarra 30-6 in round eleven to move into the top eight.

They were just as soon back out of the top eight following a 28-8 loss to the newly promoted Gold Coast side.

The Raiders ran in seven tries in a 38-10 win over Parramatta, but followed up with a 22-18 loss to Newcastle.

Another mid-season slump stymied Canberra's finals chances. They lost 28-24 to North Queensland; and 22-16 to Wests Tigers before suffering a humiliating 58-16 thumping at the hands of St George-Illawarra at Wollongong in round seventeen.

Canberra put on their best attacking display the following week; running in ten tries on their way to a 56-10 win over Gold Coast at Bruce Stadium. Michael Dobson finished the match with twenty points in a win which saw the Raiders move back to within a win of the top eight.

Any momentum gained was squashed by a 34-6 loss to Melbourne. Phil Graham scored a hat trick in a 34-30 round twenty win over Penrith, but the Raiders remained in tenth place, and their questionable defence made them unlikely finals contenders.

Canberra lost 28-22 to North Queensland before being humiliated 52-4 by Canterbury. That loss all but ended the Raiders' finals hopes.

They bounced back to beat the Warriors 26-24 before going down 30-19 to Brisbane. A 22-12 loss to Cronulla in the final round left Canberra in fourteenth spot; just one win ahead of wooden spooners Penrith.

Rookie halfback Michael Dobson was Canberra's top scorer in 2007 with 124 points. Todd Carney was their leading try scorer with twelve.

It was a tough inauguration for Neil Henry who inherited a team that had lost hundreds of games of experience. He retained his position for the 2008 season, but there was controversy ahead.

2008

Centre Joel Monaghan returned to Canberra in 2008 after a mixed stint at the Sydney Roosters. The Raiders relied mostly on their 2007 squad, but had to do without Michael Dobson and Phil Graham for much of the season due to injuries.

Adrian Purtell scored two tries in the opening round but it wasn't enough to prevent a 30-14 loss to Newcastle.

Canberra beat Penrith 20-16 in round two; and played their first home game against St George-Illawarra the following week. Joel Monaghan scored a double to help set up a 21-14 victory.

A 32-12 away loss to Gold Coast followed; but the Raiders bounced back to beat Wests Tigers 30-24 at Bruce Stadium, thanks to a hat trick from Purtell.

In round six, Canberra went down 23-16 to premiers Melbourne in a valiant effort. They had the bye the next week which left them on the cusp of the top eight, but went down 14-6 to the Warriors in round eight.

Canberra were crushed 30-4 by Sydney Roosters in round nine; but stayed in touch with the top eight when Joel Monaghan scored two of their seven tries in a 38-10 home win over South Sydney.

The Raiders had another bye in round eleven, but were comprehensively beaten 31-18 at home by Manly the following week. A 30-12 loss to Parramatta left Canberra in twelfth spot.

In a major upset, Canberra beat Brisbane 34-16 in round fourteen. Winger Justin Carney scored two of the Raiders' six tries.

The upset win over the Broncos was nothing compared to Canberra's win over Canterbury the following week. Colin Best scored four tries as the Raiders ran in eleven on their way to a 58-18 thumping of the Bulldogs in Sydney. The win saw Canberra grab a five way share of eighth spot.

Canberra went down 36-24 to high fliers Cronulla, and 30-14 to premiership leaders Melbourne to be back in twelfth spot at the end of round seventeen.

Two tries from Adrian Purtell and a field goal from Todd Carney helped Canberra to a 19-12 win over

St George-Illawarra to keep their finals chances alive.

In round nineteen, Joel Monaghan and Marshall Chalk both scored two tries as Canberra beat Sydney Roosters 34-12 to move within a point of the top eight.

After the win Todd Carney was suspended by the club for disciplinary reasons. He wouldn't play another game for the club, but later resurrected his career at the Roosters.

Marc Herbert stepped into the halfback role for the round twenty match against Gold Coast, and scored one of Canberra's eight tries in a 46-4 thumping. Terry Campese took over the goal kicking and finished the match with fourteen points. The win saw the Raiders sneak into the top eight.

Canberra again fell out of the top eight after being smashed 34-6 by Brisbane. The poor result gave no indication of what would happen the following week.

In round 22 Canberra faced Penrith at Bruce Stadium. The Panthers were a point ahead of Canberra on the table as several sides battled for a spot in the top eight.

In the best attacking display in Canberra's history, they scored a staggering thirteen tries on their way to a record 74-12 victory.

Terry Campese scored four tries and finished the match with 36 points; just two short of Mal Meninga's club record. Unheralded interchange player Trevor Thurling finished with a hat trick in the win which saw the Raiders move up to sixth spot.

Canberra built on their momentum with a 38-18 win over Newcastle. Fullback David Milne scored two of the Raiders' seven tries.

In round 24, Canberra scored seven tries to four in a 40-25 win over Souths to stay in sixth place. They lost 22-10 to North Queensland the following week, but finished the season by gaining their revenge on Canterbury; beating the Bulldogs 52-34 at Bruce Stadium in a match which produced sixteen tries, including hat tricks to David Milne and Joel Monaghan.

Canberra finished the season in sixth spot, and faced Cronulla in their qualifying final. The Sharks scored seven tries, including a hat trick to winger Misi Taulapapa in their 36-10 win which ended Canberra's season.

Terry Campese was Canberra's top scorer with 120, ahead of Todd Carney on 110. Adrian Purtell was the club's leading try scorer with fifteen; one ahead of Joel Monaghan.

2009

Former Clive Churchill Medal winner and Canberra stalwart David Furner replaced Neil Henry for the 2009 season. Furner introduced a number of new players into first grade during the season including forwards David Shillington and Shaun Fensom, halfback Josh McCrone, goal kicking centre Jarrod Croker, blockbusting winger Daniel Vidot, and fullback Josh Dugan.

Winger Justin Carney scored two tries for Canberra in their opening match against Wests Tigers but it wasn't enough to prevent a 34-26 defeat.

The Raiders were thumped 28-4 by Sydney Roosters in round two to slump to the bottom of the table. An 18-16 loss to Parramatta kept them in last place.

Canberra broke through for their first win of the season in round four, beating North Queensland by 23-18. A 24-14 win over Cronulla the following week saw them grab a six way share of eighth place.

In round six Canberra went down 16-10 to Gold Coast; and further losses followed. They went down 30-20 to Canterbury; and 18-10 to Penrith to be in second last spot before having the bye in round nine.

Canberra conceded eight tries in a 46-6 thumping by Melbourne; but bounced back when Jarrod Croker and David Milne crossed for doubles in their 38-12 win over the Warriors.

Canberra scored six tries to four in their 34-18 win over Souths in round twelve to move within two wins of the top eight.

The Raiders had the bye in round thirteen and turned the halfway mark of the competition in eleventh spot.

After the break, Canberra were unlucky to go down 24-22 to Cronulla; before falling 20-14 to Manly at Brookvale Oval.

Justin Carney and Joel Monaghan both scored doubles as Canberra beat Melbourne 26-16 in round sixteen; and a 34-28 win over Gold Coast the following week kept the Raiders in touch with the top eight.

Canberra were beaten 23-4 by Newcastle; and 27-14 by Penrith; and 25-4 by Wests Tigers to all but end their chances of making the finals.

In round 21 the Raiders hosted Brisbane at Bruce Stadium. No one could have predicted Canberra running in ten tries on their way to a 56-0 victory. Phil Graham scored four tries, while Terry Campese kicked eight goals.

The following week Canberra went down 23-20 to Canterbury. A 24-12 win over St George-Illawarra followed before a 34-20 loss to the Warriors.

In the second last round of the season, Phil Graham scored two of Canberra's five tries in a 30-14 win over Newcastle. The Raiders finished the season with a 22-10 loss to Brisbane, and ended the year in thirteenth place.

Terry Campese was again the club's top point scorer with 129. Rookie Jarrod Croker was Canberra's top try scorer with twelve; two ahead of Joel Monaghan and Phil Graham.

2010

Canberra went into the 2010 season with the same squad as the previous year. Their young team improved as they gained experience, with David Shillington, Josh Dugan and Jarrod Croker becoming stars of the competition.

The Raiders started shakily; going down 34-16 to Penrith. In front of their home crowd, Canberra had a hard fought 22-14 win over Brisbane in round two. Halfback Josh McCrone scored a double for the Raiders.

Canberra were smashed 24-4 by Gold Coast before going down 35-22 to Wests Tigers at home. At the end of round four they were at the bottom of the ladder.

In round five, Canberra upset Parramatta 24-14; but were smashed 36-6 by Sydney Roosters the following week. The big story after round six was Melbourne being stripped of competition points due to salary cap breaches; opening up another spot in the finals.

Canberra were beaten 26-24 at home by Souths; but then upset the Warriors in New Zealand 23-16. They had the bye in round nine, and were two points short of the top eight.

Melbourne continued to fire despite having nothing to play for, and beat Canberra 17-6 at Bruce Stadium in round ten.

Canberra bounced back with a 22-14 win over St George-Illawarra in Wollongong; and enjoyed a week off with their second bye.

In round thirteen, Canberra scored five tries to four in a 28-24 win over Gold Coast. At the halfway mark of the competition, the Raiders sat in tenth spot.

The Raiders went down 16-8 to lowly North Queensland; and were disappointing in an 18-8 loss to Wests Tigers at Leichhardt the following week. They continued to struggle in attack, and were beaten 18-10 by Canterbury to fall four points behind the top eight.

The Raiders went down 22-10 to Sydney Roosters in round seventeen before causing a boil over by beating Manly 24-22 at Brookvale.

Canberra's attack finally clicked in round nineteen. They scored nine tries, including a hat trick to Josh Dugan, as they romped home 52-18 against Newcastle. Daniel Vidot also crossed for a double in the win.

Vidot again scored two tries as Canberra beat Cronulla 20-13 at Bruce Stadium. They were smashed 30-12 by Melbourne the following week.

The Raiders kept their slim finals chances alive in round 22 by beating Penrith 30-26. The following week they scored five tries to three in a 28-14 win over Canterbury in Sydney.

Canberra ran in six tries in a 32-16 home win over St George-Illawarra which saw the Raiders join Brisbane in equal eighth spot with two rounds to play.

Rookie winger Reece Robinson scored four tries, and Josh Dugan crossed for a double as Canberra crushed North Queensland 48-4 in the second last round.

In the last round of the season, a crowd of almost 40,000 packed Lang Park to watch Brisbane take on Canberra. The Raiders snuck home 18-16 on the back of a double to Daniel Vidot to finish in seventh spot; and deny Brisbane a place in the finals for the first time since 1991.

Canberra faced Penrith on the Panthers' home turf in the qualifying final. Penrith had finished in second place, and went into the match as strong favourites. Both sides scored four tries, but the accurate goal kicking of Jarrod Croker gave Canberra a 24-22 upset win.

The Raiders advanced to a semi-final against West Tigers at Bruce Stadium. The Tigers had suffered a 19-15 loss to Sydney Roosters in golden point the previous week. In another exciting game, both sides scored four tries, but it was a penalty goal to Benji Marshall that separated the sides, with the Tigers running out 26-24 winners.

Canberra had performed above expectations in 2010. Jarrod Croker was their top point scorer with 126, while Terry Campese contributed 80. Daniel Vidot was the club's leading try scorer with sixteen; three ahead of fullback Josh Dugan.

The promising finish to the 2010 season augured well for the future of the club, with coach David Furner gaining a reputation for bringing the best out of young players.

2011

Canberra benefited from the Melbourne salary cap scandal by signing front row forward Brett White for the 2011 season. The Raiders also picked up former Manly premiership winning halfback Matt Orford, but he only played a handful of games before suffering an injury.

The Raiders continued to find impressive young players such as half Sam Williams, centre or winger Blake Ferguson and forward Josh Papalii. However, the club had to compete without Terry Campese for almost the whole season.

Canberra started the season on fire, running in seven tries on their way to a 40-12 win over Cronulla at Bruce Stadium.

The Raiders came back to earth in round two; going down at home 20-4 to Brisbane. The next week they conceded six tries in a 34-24 loss to Wests Tigers at Campbelltown. Blake Ferguson scored a hat trick to give Canberra fans something to cheer.

In round four, Canberra went down 23-22 to Gold Coast in golden point extra time after Greg Bird kicked the winning field goal.

The Raiders were comprehensively beaten 36-10 by Penrith, and slumped to equal last place alongside Gold Coast.

In round six Canberra lost their fifth match in a row; beaten 26-18 away by North Queensland. The Raiders were on their own at the bottom of the ladder.

A 22-12 loss to Newcastle followed; and in round eight Canberra were smashed 49-12 by Wests Tigers at Bruce Stadium. The Raiders conceded eight tries in the loss.

Canberra's attack hit rock bottom in round nine when they were beaten 20-0 by Manly at Brookvale.

The Raiders produced a stunning upset in round ten, defeating Melbourne 20-12. The following week they defeated Canterbury by the same score, but were still on the bottom of the ladder.

Canberra had the bye in round twelve which seemed to stall their momentum, as they were beaten 40-24 by North Queensland the following week.

In their second golden point loss of the season, Canberra went down 25-24 to Brisbane at Lang Park. Peter Wallace kicked the winning field goal.

Canberra had another bye in round fifteen, and finally moved away from the bottom of the table by beating Parramatta 25-12. Sam Williams scored twice for the Raiders.

In round seventeen, Jarrod Croker scored two tries and eighteen points as Canberra thrashed Sydney Roosters 38-12 at the Sydney Football Stadium.

Canberra went down 26-12 to Cronulla; and 26-0 to Melbourne; all but ending any chance of the Raiders making the finals.

Josh Dugan scored a double in a 24-19 win over St George-Illawarra; before going down 29-10 to the Warriors, and 40-8 at Newcastle.

Canberra conceded eight tries in a 47-18 loss to Souths at Bruce Stadium as their season unravelled. A 26-18 loss to Gold Coast followed; and a Luke Walsh field goal denied the Raiders as they went down 19-18 to Penrith.

The Raiders finished their season with six consecutive losses, as they went down 36-22 to Canterbury. Canberra finished fifteenth, and only avoided the wooden spoon on percentages.

Jarrod Croker was the club's top scorer with 154, while Blake Ferguson was far and away their leading try scorer with thirteen.

2012

Canberra signed veteran utility Shaun Berrigan for the 2012 season. Berrigan won the Clive Churchill Medal while playing for Brisbane in 2006; and could play anywhere in the backline, as well as hooker.

David Furner unveiled more young players including utility back Jack Wighton and electrifying winger Edrick Lee. However, club stalwart Alan Tongue retired at the end of the 2011 season after playing 220 first grade matches for the club.

The Raiders had lacked consistency for several years, and were looking to vastly improve on their disappointing 2011 season.

Canberra started the season with a 24-19 loss to Melbourne at Bruce Stadium in a tough encounter. Jarrod Croker scored a double in round two as the Raiders got their season underway with a 24-12 away win over Gold Coast.

The Raiders went down 14-8 in round three, but bounced back to beat Wests Tigers 30-16 at Campbelltown, thanks to eighteen points from Jarrod Croker.

Canberra went down 22-6 to North Queensland, as their season looked to again be synonymous with inconsistency.

In round six, Reece Robinson and Jarrod Croker both scored two tries as the Raiders ran in seven in a 32-12 win over the Warriors. The win saw Canberra move back into the top eight after three wins and three losses.

Canberra were belted 30-6 by Brisbane, and conceded eight tries in a 44-22 loss to Cronulla, to slump back to thirteenth spot.

An 18-12 loss to Manly followed; but the Raiders returned to the winners list with a 40-34 win over Parramatta at Bruce Stadium in round ten. Reece Robinson and second row forward Joel Thompson both crossed for doubles.

Canberra had the bye in round eleven, before losing 36-18 to Souths. The Raiders hit rock bottom in round thirteen when they were thumped 40-0 at home by Wests Tigers. They were in second last spot at the halfway mark of the season.

The unpredictable Raiders bounced back the next week by beating Newcastle 32-16, with Edrick Lee scoring two tries.

After another bye, Canberra were belted 40-18 by North Queensland. In round seventeen, the Raiders beat St George-Illawarra 22-18; and then thrashed top of the table Melbourne 40-12 in a major upset. Lee scored a hat trick in the win.

Canberra conceded eight tries in a 38-26 loss to Gold Coast at home; but typically bounced back with a 36-4 away win over Cronulla. Jarrod Croker scored two tries and finished the game with twenty points.

The Raiders were smashed 36-6 at home by Newcastle before beating Brisbane 28-12 on the back of a double from Josh Dugan. With four rounds to play the Raiders were still a chance of making the finals.

Canberra beat Penrith 20-10 in round 23, and snuck home 24-20 against Sydney Roosters the following week to join Brisbane and Wests Tigers in equal seventh spot.

In the second last round, winger Sandor Earl scored a hat trick, and Reece Robinson crossed for a double as Canberra smashed Canterbury 34-6 at Bruce Stadium. The win saw the Raiders in outright seventh place.

In the final round, Canberra went to New Zealand, and beat the Warriors 42-22. Blake Ferguson and Reece Robinson both scored two tries in the win which saw the Raiders finish the season in sixth place.

In the elimination final, Canberra faced Cronulla in front of almost 25,000 fans at Bruce Stadium. The Raiders were at their attacking best, scoring seven tries on their way to a comprehensive 34-16 victory. Sandor Earl and Blake Ferguson both scored doubles for the Raiders.

Canberra moved on to a semi-final showdown against Souths in Sydney. The Rabbitohs proved too strong, scoring six tries to three in a 38-16 win which ended Canberra's season.

The Raiders had unexpectedly returned to the finals in 2012 after finishing equal last the previous year. They were still plagued by inconsistency; but had a solid core of players that were steadily improving.

Jarrod Croker was the top scorer for Canberra with 226. It was enough to also be the leading scorer in the competition. Croker was also the club's leading try scorer with sixteen; equal with Blake Ferguson.

2013

David Furner continued to produce promising young players in 2013, with Joel Edwards, Anthony Milford and Paul Vaughan all making their first grade debuts.

Canberra started poorly in 2013; going down 32-10 to Penrith in the opening round of the season. Shortly after the match fullback Josh Dugan was sensationally sacked from the club after an off field incident. Blake Ferguson was suspended by the club for his role in the same incident. Dugan would later resurrect his career at St George-Illawarra.

The drama surrounding the club affected the on field performance, with the Raiders getting smashed 36-0 by Gold Coast in round two.

Reece Robinson moved to fullback and scored two tries as Canberra beat St George-Illawarra 30-17 in round three to get their season back on track. Jarrod Croker also scored two tries in the win, and finished the match with eighteen points.

Canberra went down 28-12 at Newcastle in round four, and found themselves on the bottom of the table.

They snuck home 24-22 against Sydney Roosters, and were back in the finals hunt after beating the Warriors 20-16 at Bruce Stadium.

Canberra went down 30-12 to North Queensland before upsetting top of the table Melbourne 24-20 in round eight.

The Raiders moved into the top eight for the first time after smashing Newcastle 44-14. Sandor Earl and Blake Ferguson both scored hat tricks in the win.

Another season of inconsistency weighed on Canberra, as they went down 30-20 to Cronulla, and 16-10 to Manly to fall outside of the top eight. They had a bye in round twelve, and beat Brisbane 30-18 to be in eighth spot at the halfway mark of the season.

Canberra beat Penrith 24-12; but again struggled to string wins together. They lost 17-12 to Wests Tigers in round fifteen; and were crushed 32-2 by competition leaders South Sydney the following week.

Canberra bounced back with a 26-18 win over North Queensland before enjoying their second bye. They then beat Parramatta 14-0 to move back into the top eight.

In round twenty, Canberra travelled to Wollongong to face a St George-Illawarra team featuring Josh Dugan. The Raiders ran out winners by 22-18.

Despite being in a fight to secure a spot in the finals; Canberra turned in one of their worst ever performances in round 21 against Melbourne at Bruce Stadium. They conceded twelve tries as Melbourne romped to a 68-4 victory.

The Raiders went down 28-22 to Sydney Roosters to again fall out of the top eight; and a 28-16 loss to Canterbury put their chances in deep jeopardy. David Furner was sacked as coach, and replaced by Andrew Dunemann for the rest of the season.

Canberra lost 36-22 to Manly at Bruce Stadium in round 24 to drop to twelfth place; although they were still mathematically able to make the finals.

In the second last round Jarrod Croker scored a hat trick, but it was not enough to stop a 50-16 mauling at the hands of the Warriors. Shortly after the match Blake Ferguson was sacked from the club for another off field indiscretion.

The season came to a merciful end with a 38-18 loss to Cronulla. The Raiders finished in thirteenth spot.

Jarrod Croker scored 136 points, while Blake Ferguson was the club's leading try scorer with ten; one ahead of Sandor Earl and Anthony Milford.

Former premiership winning halfback and Clive Churchill Medal winner Ricky Stuart came back to Canberra in 2014 as head coach. Stuart had won a premiership with Sydney Roosters in 2002.

Without Josh Dugan and Blake Ferguson, the club was again faced with going through a rebuilding stage; but were fortunate to retain the core of their side, led by Jarrod Croker.

2014

When Ricky Stuart announced he was leaving Parramatta to join Canberra as coach for the 2014 season, the Raiders squad was settled. They lost Tom Learoyd-Lahrs, who had struggled with injury for much of the previous season.

Canberra began their season with a 28-22 away loss to North Queensland; before Jarrod Croker scored two tries in a 26-20 away win over Newcastle.

In round three, the Raiders played their first game at home. They were beaten 24-12 by Gold Coast in an upset; but characteristically bounced back to beat Souths in Sydney 30-18 the following week.

Canberra lost 12-6 to Penrith and then went down 26-12 to Newcastle; just a month after beating the Knights. The loss saw the Raiders just one win ahead of last placed Cronulla.

Reece Robinson scored two tries as Canberra upset Melbourne 24-22 in round seven. Any thoughts of a return to form were dispelled when they were crushed 54-18 by Manly at Brookvale the following week.

Canberra's defence was again lacking in round nine. They were thumped 54-12 by the Warriors, and followed up with a 26-20 home loss to Penrith.

Typically, Canberra bounced back in round eleven by beating North Queensland 42-12 at Bruce Stadium. Jack Wighton scored two of Canberra's seven tries, and Jarrod Croker finished the match with eighteen points.

The Raiders were beaten 26-12 by Sydney Roosters; and 28-4 by Brisbane, to be in fourteenth place at the midway point of the season.

The club had a much needed bye in round fourteen; but then lost 22-14 to Canterbury. When Wests Tigers beat the Raiders 19-18 at Campbelltown, Canberra were left in a share of last spot on the ladder with Cronulla and Newcastle.

After their second bye, Canberra bounced back with a 36-20 away win over Gold Coast on the back of two tries from fullback Anthony Milford.

A 28-14 loss to Melbourne followed, and when they were beaten 34-18 by Souths, the Raiders were again locked in a battle for the wooden spoon.

For the second time in 2014, the Raiders let in 54 points against the Warriors. Their round 21 match at Bruce Stadium ended in a 54-18 win for the away team.

Canberra lost 18-10 to Parramatta; and 34-16 to St George-Illawarra; and the end of the season could not come quickly enough.

In the battle for the wooden spoon, Canberra beat Cronulla 22-12 at Endeavour Field in round 24. Anthony Milford, nor playing five-eighth, scored two of Canberra's four tries.

Canberra ensured they would avoid the wooden spoon by beating Wests Tigers 27-12 at Bruce Stadium in the second last round.

A miserable season ended on a positive note when the Raiders beat Parramatta 33-20; but they still finished second last.

Jarrod Croker scored 202 points, and was also the club's top try scorer with eighteen.

2015

Canberra were more active in the player transfer market at the end of the 2014 than they had been in several years, as Ricky Stuart started to put his own stamp on the club.

Long serving five-eighth Terry Campese, and front row forward Brett White retired from the NRL. Reece Robinson joined Parramatta, and young utility back Anthony Milford joined Brisbane.

English hooker Josh Hodgson joined the club, as did former New Zealand internationals Iosia Soliola and Frank-Paul Nu'uausala. Centre Joey Leilua came from Newcastle, while utility player Blake Austin moved from Wests Tigers.

Jack Wighton was given first crack at the fullback spot, and scored two tries in the opening round to help Canberra to a 24-20 away win over Cronulla.

Canberra went down 18-6 to the Warriors in the first home game; and then went down 22-20 to St George-Illawarra. A 34-6 thumping at the hands of Sydney Roosters inspired little faith in the Canberra fans.

In round five, Canberra played Manly in the first premiership match played in Albury. The Raiders scored five tries in a 29-16 victory to get their season back on track.

Canberra narrowly went down 14-10 to Melbourne before beating Wests Tigers 30-22 at Leichhardt, as the season started to look like the familiar pattern of inconsistency.

In round eight, Canberra faced Souths in the unfamiliar territory of Cairns. Winger Edrick Lee scored two of the Raiders' six tries in a 30-22 win.

The Raiders were at their attacking best in round nine; scoring ten tries in a 56-16 blitz over Gold Coast. Blake Austin scored a double, as did Jarrod Croker, who finished the match with 24 points. The win saw Canberra break into the top eight for the first time in the season.

Canberra's defence was called into question after a 32-18 loss to St George-Illawarra, and a 41-34 loss to Canterbury. The defeats saw the Raiders fall out of the top eight.

A 24-12 loss to Brisbane followed, but the Raiders broke their losing streak with a 44-22 win over Newcastle in round thirteen, with Blake Austin and Edrick Lee both scoring two tries, and Jarrod Croker racking up twenty points.

At the midway point of the season Canberra were sitting in ninth place. They had a bye in round fourteen, and were beaten 21-20 by North Queensland thanks to a Johnathan Thurston field goal the following week.

A 30-8 loss to the Warriors was followed by a much needed bye. When Blake Austin scored a hat trick as Canberra again beat Newcastle 36-22 in round eighteen, they were still a fair chance of challenging for the finals.

The Raiders went down 21-20 to Cronulla in golden point in round nineteen; but beat Penrith 34-24 on their home turf thanks to doubles from Paul Vaughan and rookie winger Jordan Rapana.

Canberra fell 32-24 to the premiership leading North Queensland before going down 20-18 at home to Wests Tigers to place their finals chances in jeopardy.

In round 23 they were beaten 26-24 by a desperate Manly side at Bruce Stadium, and were four points short of the top eight with just three rounds to play.

A 28-12 loss to Gold Coast the following week ended Canberra's chances of making the finals. They bounced back to score six tries in a 34-18 win over Penrith in their last home game of the year.

In the final round, Jarrod Croker scored two tries in Canberra's 28-24 golden point win over Parramatta. The Raiders finished tenth; two wins short of making the finals.

Jarrod Croker was again the Raiders' top point scorer with 236. He was second to James Maloney as the competition's leading scorer. Blake Austin was the club's top try scorer with fourteen; two ahead of Croker and Edrick Lee.

2016

Canberra signed Gold Coast halfback Aidan Sezer for the 2016 season. His combination with five-eighth Blake Austin would provide the club's exciting young backline with attacking opportunities.

Another English forward, Elliot Whitehead joined the club, as did Newcastle hooker Adam Clydesdale and veteran forward Jeff Lima. Prop forward Shannon Boyd became a key player in the squad, especially after the mid-season departure of Frank-Paul Nu'uausala.

Canberra opened their season with a 30-22 win over Penrith at Bruce Stadium. New halfback Aidan Sezer scored two of five tries in the victory.

In round two, barnstorming forward Josh Papalii scored twice, and Sam Williams kicked a decisive field goal in a 21-20 victory over Sydney Roosters.

Not even golden point extra time could separate Canberra and Newcastle in round three, with the game finishing in a 24-24 draw.

Canberra suffered their first loss of the season in round four, going down 24-20 to Gold Coast. They recovered to beat Canterbury 22-8 at Belmore on the back of eighteen points from Jarrod Croker.

In round six Canberra produced their worst performance of the season; going down 36-6 to Parramatta. A 40-16 thumping by Cronulla the following week saw the Raiders fall to seventh spot.

After two humiliating losses, Canberra were fired up for their home match against Wests Tigers in round eight. They ran in eleven tries, including four to Jordan Rapana as they crushed Wests Tigers by 60-6.

In round nine Canberra played Penrith at Bathurst. In an exciting match, Penrith prevailed 19-18. When Canberra went down 16-12 to St George-

Illawarra at Kogarah the following week, the Raiders slipped out of the top eight for the first time all season.

Canberra continued to bring the NRL to new areas in round eleven when their match against the Warriors was played in Taranaki. The Raiders scored six tries to two in a 38-12 win, with Jarrod Croker notching eighteen points.

The Raiders beat Canterbury 32-20 in round twelve; and a 30-18 home win over Manly saw them turn the midway point of the season in sixth spot.

Canberra went down 28-14 to Brisbane in round fourteen before enjoying the bye week. They returned to beat Gold Coast 30-22 thanks to two tries each from Jarrod Croker and winger Brenko Lee. For the second time in the season, the match between Canberra and Newcastle went to golden point extra time. This time Canberra got home by 29-25.

Canberra moved up to fifth spot in round eighteen when they beat premiers North Queensland 26-12 at Bruce Stadium. Jack Wighton scored two tries in the win. A second bye and a 26-22 win over the Warriors saw Canberra break into the top four by the end of round twenty. They consolidated their spot by scoring ten tries in a 54-4 thumping of Souths.

Canberra knocked Cronulla from the top of the table in round 22 with a 30-14 win at Endeavour Field. Jarrod Croker kicked seven goals in the win which saw the Raiders move up to third spot.

The Raiders established their premiership credentials by beating the new premiership leaders, Melbourne, 22-8 in round 23.

Canberra made it eight wins in a row by coming from behind to beat Parramatta 28-18 on the back of four tries from Brenko Lee.

Jordan Rapana scored three of Canberra's eight tries in a 44-30 away win over Manly, and they finished in second spot after beating Wests Tigers 52-10 at Leichhardt in the final round. Josh Papalii and Jordan Rapana each scored two of Canberra's nine tries.

The Raiders were strong favourites going into their clash with Cronulla in the first week of the finals. However, they lost hooker Josh Hodgson to injury early in the match. Both sides scored two tries, but a late penalty goal to James Maloney gave the Sharks a 16-14 win.

Canberra recovered to face Penrith the following week, and welcomed back Blake Austin from injury. Josh Hodgson defied the odds to also take his place.

Tries to Jordan Rapana, Jarrod Croker and Blake Austin set up an 18-0 lead early in the second half, and the Raiders resisted a second half fight back from Penrith to run out winners 22-12. Jarrod Croker scored fourteen points in the victory which saw Canberra within a win of the Grand Final.

Canberra came up against Melbourne in the Grand Final qualifier. Cameron Smith kicked an early penalty goal, but Canberra went ahead through a try to Jordan Rapana.

A try from Cooper Cronk just before halftime gave Melbourne an 8-6 lead at the break. They went ahead 14-6 before Canberra hit back through a try to Elliott Whitehead. The Storm hung on to win by 14-12, ending a valiant campaign from the Raiders.

Jarrod Croker was Canberra's and the competition's leading point scorer with 296. Jordan Rapana was the competition's top try scorer with 23, equal with Melbourne winger Suliasi Vunivalu.

2017

Canberra lost prop Paul Vaughan to St George-Illawarra, but unearthed an exciting winger in Nick Cotric, who quickly earned his spot in first grade.

The Raiders opened their season with a 20-16 loss to North Queensland in golden point extra time. In round two, they were hammered 42-16 by Cronulla. They responded by smashing Wests Tigers 46-6 in their first home game. Jordan Rapana scored two of their eight tries.

After going down 13-12 to Brisbane, Canberra beat Parramatta 30-18, and Gold Coast 42-16 to move into the top eight. Jordan Rapana bagged another three tries against the Titans.

Canberra beat the Warriors 20-8, before going down 20-18 to Manly in another golden point loss. The Raiders then went down 16-10 to Canterbury, and dropped to tenth place on the ladder.

A 34-20 loss to Newcastle was followed by a 22-16 win over Parramatta which saw Canberra back in eighth spot. In round twelve, they defeated Sydney Roosters 24-16, with Jordan Rapana scoring two of their four tries.

The following week, Canberra lost in golden point for the third time in the season. They went down 21-20 to Manly, courtesy of a field goal from star halfback Daly Cherry-Evans. The loss saw the Raiders again drop out of the top eight.

Canberra went down 24-20 to Penrith in Bathurst before enjoying a much needed by week. They returned with a 30-20 loss to Brisbane, and a 31-18 defeat at the hands of North Queensland.

After a second bye round, Canberra found a golden point victory by beating St George-Illawarra 18-14. They followed up with a 20-14 loss to competition leader Melbourne, and were three wins outside of the top eight with six rounds to play.

Canberra beat Souths 32-18 to stay in touch, and followed up with a 30-12 victory over Cronulla. In round 23, Nick Cotric scored two tries in a 36-16 win over the Warriors, but Canberra remained two wins short of the top eight.

A 26-22 loss to Penrith dented Canberra's chances, and their quest to make the finals came to an end in round 25, despite beating Newcastle 46-28. Jordan Rapana scored three tries against the Knights.

In the final round, Canberra were thumped 32-6 by Melbourne. They finished in tenth place, two wins short of the top eight. Jordan Rapana was their leading try scorer for the season with 21. Jarrod Croker was again their top point scorer with 190.

2018

Canberra went into the 2018 season with mostly the same squad that disappointingly missed out on playing finals football in 2017.

A nail biting 30-28 loss to Gold Coast in the opening round was followed by a 30-28 loss to Newcastle. Canberra went down 20-19 to the Warriors, and 32-16 to Manly to be equal last without a win after four rounds.

Canberra finally found a win in round five, beating Canterbury 26-10. The Raiders then beat Parramatta 18-2, but were smashed 42-22 by Souths in Gosford in round seven.

A tough 18-8 away win over North Queensland was followed by a 32-18 win over Gold Coast. Canberra went down 24-16 to Cronulla, and 25-18 to St George-Illawarra before sneaking home 21-20 against Manly, thanks to a field goal from halfback Aidan Sezer.

After a bye round, Canberra were pipped 23-22 by Penrith. They responded by smashing Wests Tigers 48-12. Joseph Tapine and Joey Leilua both scored two tries in the win.

Canberra went down 26-22 to Brisbane, before beating Canterbury 32-28. The Raiders were in ninth spot with eight rounds to play.

Veteran winger Michael Oldfield scored three tries in a 38-12 win over North Queensland. The Raiders then went down 28-24 to Cronulla, and were smashed 44-10 by competition leaders Melbourne.

A 40-31 loss to Penrith in round 21 ended Canberra's hopes of making the finals. The Raiders lost 22-20 to Wests Tigers, before upsetting Sydney Roosters 14-12 on the back of five goals from halfback Sam Williams.

Canberra beat Souths 24-12 before losing 20-16 to the Warriors in the final round. The Raiders ended the season in tenth place, five wins short of the top eight. Joey Leilua was the club's leading try scorer for the season with fourteen. Jarrod Croker was Canberra's top point scorer for the year with 154.

2019

Junior Paulo left Canberra at the end of 2018 to continue his career at Parramatta, while Blake Austin moved to England. Young backs Bayley Simonsson and Charnze Nicoll-Klokstad became regular first graders during the 2019 season.

Canberra began their campaign with a solid 21-0 win over Gold Coast. They went down 22-10 to 2018 runners up Melbourne, before beating Newcastle 17-10 and North Queensland 30-12.

After beating Parramatta 19-0, Canberra defeated Brisbane 26-22. In round seven, they lost 24-20 to Manly, but remained in the top four.

A 30-12 win over Penrith was followed by a 30-24 loss to defending premiers Sydney Roosters. Canberra went down 16-12 to Souths, and 22-16 to North Queensland, before beating Canterbury by 12-10 to be in fifth place at the halfway mark of their season.

Canberra belted Wests Tigers 28-0 to move back into the top four. They snuck home 22-20 against Cronulla, but went down 22-16 to Parramatta in Darwin. A bye week in round 16 kept Canberra in the top four.

Charnze Nicoll-Kolokstad scored two of Canberra's seven tries in a 36-14 win over St George-Illawarra. The Raiders then beat Wests Tigers 20-12, Penrith 30-18, and the Warriors 46-12.

In round 21, Canberra went down 22-18 to Sydney Roosters. The following week they upset competition leader Melbourne 22-18. Jarrod Croker scored two tries against the Storm.

Canberra went down 18-14 to Manly before beating Cronulla 15-14 in golden point, thanks to a field goal from Aidan Sezer.

In the final round, Canberra went down 24-20 to the Warriors, and finished in fourth place. They faced minor premiers Melbourne in the first week of the finals, and produced a stunning 12-10 upset.

Canberra faced Souths in a Grand Final Qualifier. The Raiders finished 16-10 victors to advance to the Grand Final for the first time since 1994.

Canberra faced Sydney Roosters in the Grand Final. Their team for the decider was Charnze Nicoll-Kolokstad, Nick Cotric, Jarrod Croker (C), Joey Leilua, Jordan Rapana, Jack Wighton, Aidan Sezer, Joseph Tapine, Elliott Whitehead, John Bateman, Iosia Soliola, Josh Hodgson, Josh Papalii. Interchange: Emre Guler, Corey Horsburgh, Bailey Simonsson, Dunamis Lui. Coahc: Ricky Stuart.

Canberra were denied an early scoring opportunity when a charge down ricocheted off a Sydney Roosters trainer. Shortly afterwards, Sam Verrills scored for the Roosters to open the scoring.

Jack Wighton crossed for Canberra, and the Raiders went into the halftime break behind 8-6. A Jarrod Croker penalty goal levelled the scores at 8-8 ten minutes into the second half.

With less than ten minutes to go, Canberra recovered the ball from a kick as the referee signalled six more tackles. The ruling was overturned, and the Roosters posted a try to Daniel Tupou which proved the difference in a 14-8 win.

Jack Wighton was awarded the Clive Churchill Medal for being the best player on the field in the Grand Final.

Jarrod Croker was Canberra's leading try scorer for the season with thirteen. Croker was also the Raiders' top point scorer for the year with 228.

Canberra farewelled Joey Leilua at the end of the season. Leilua opted to continue his career with Wests Tigers. The Raiders also lost Aidan Sezer, who continued his career with Huddersfield in the English Super League.

2020

The 2020 competition was like no other. The impact of the COVID-19 virus saw the entire competition restructured with clubs living inside safety bubbles. The season was played over 20 rounds with home ground advantages lost.

Canberra began their 2020 campaign with a 24-6 win over Gold Coast. Jack Wighton scored two tries against the Titans.

The Raiders beat the Warriors 20-6, and Melbourne 22-6 before going down 34-18 to Newcastle in round four.

Canberra bounced back to beat Wests Tigers 14-6, but went down 14-6 to Manly, and 25-24 to Parramatta in golden point to be in seventh place after seven rounds.

Canberra bounced back to beat St George-Illawarra 22-16; but went down 20-14 to Melbourne in round nine. The following week, Canberra beat Sydney Roosters 24-20, and sat in sixth place at the halfway mark of the competition.

The Raiders beat Souths 18-12, and North Queensland 14-12, before going down 28-12 to Penrith. In round fourteen, they smashed Brisbane 36-8, with Nick Cotric scoring two of their six tries.

Nick Cotric and Jack Wighton both scored two tries in a 36-16 win over Gold Coast which saw Canberra in fifth place with five rounds to play.

Tom Starling and Jack Wighton each scored two tries in a 34-20 win over Canterbury; but an 18-6 loss to Sydney Roosters cruelled Canberra's chances of finishing in the top four.

Jack Wighton scored two tries in a 37-8 thumping of St George-Illawarra in round eighteen. Canberra beat the Warriors 26-14, and Cronulla 38-28 to finish in fifth place.

Canberra faced eighth placed Cronulla in the first week of the finals. Jack Wighton and George Williams each scored two tries in a 32-20 victory.

The Raiders kept their season alive by beating Sydney Roosters 22-18 in their semi-final. Canberra advanced to a Grand Final qualifier, but were thumped 30-10 by eventual premiers Melbourne.

Nick Cotric was Canberra's leading try scorer for the season with fourteen, one more than Jack Wighton. Jarrod Croker was again the club's leading point scorer for the year with 162.

2021

Nick Cotric left Canberra at the end of 2020 to join Canterbury. The Raiders kept the rest of their main squad, but lost halfback George Williams midway through the year when he opted to return to England to play for Warrington.

Canberra began their season with a 30-12 win over Wests Tigers. Jordan Rapana scored two tries in the win.

The Raiders beat Cronulla 12-10, before going down 34-31 to the Warriors. After beating Gold Coast 20-4, Canberra were belted 30-10 by Penrith and fell to eighth place.

Canberra were thrashed 35-10 by Parramatta, before going down 26-24 to North Queensland; 34-20 to Souths, and 24-16 to Newcastle.

In round ten, Canberra broke their losing streak by beating Canterbury 20-18. The win moved the Raiders back into the top eight.

A 34-10 belting from Melbourne was followed by a 44-16 thumping from Sydney Roosters. At the midway point of the season, Canberra had slumped to fourteenth place.

After a bye round, Canberra beat Brisbane 38-16 to stay in touch with the top eight. They went down 22-20 to St George-Illawarra, before being hammered 44-6 by Gold Coast.

Canberra bounced back to upset Manly 20-16, thanks to two tries from Sam Williams. The Raiders followed up with a 34-18 win over Cronulla, and were on the cusp of the top eight with seven rounds to play.

After sneaking home 12-10 against Parramatta, Canberra went down 34-24 to Newcastle, and missed an opportunity to move into the eight.

Canberra beat St George-Illawarra 20-12, before going down 26-16 to Melbourne, and 19-18 to Manly. A 28-16 win over the Warriors left the Raiders with some hope going into the final round.

Canberra were belted 40-16 by Sydney Roosters and finished the season in tenth place. They missed the finals on for and against.

Jordan Rapana was Canberra's top try scorer for the season with twelve. Jarrod Croker was the club's leading point scorer for the year with 80.

2022

Nick Cotric returned to Canberra in 2022 after a season with Canterbury. He was joined by Bulldogs' teammate Adam Elliott, and Gold Coast halfback Jamal Fogarty, who missed most of the opening round due to injury.

Canberra began their season with a 24-19 victory over Cronulla; but the following week they were well beaten 26-6 by North Queensland.

Centre Matthew Timoko scored tries as the Raiders snuck home 24-22 against Gold Coast, before they were defeated 25-6 by Manly in Mudgee.

In round five, Canberra travelled to Wagga Wagga, but lost 30-16 to Melbourne. An 18-12 home loss to North Queensland the following week left the Raiders in twelfth spot with just two wins from their first six games.

After being pummelled 36-6 by defending premiers Penrith, Canberra were left heartbroken following a 21-20 golden point loss to NZ Warriors. After eight rounds they were in a five way tie for last place.

A solid 14-4 win over Canterbury was followed by a 30-10 upset win over Cronulla at Lang Park. The Raiders then belted Souths 32-12 in Dubbo to move to the cusp of the top eight. A 28-20 loss to Parramatta left them in tenth spot at the midway point of the competition.

Canberra upset Sydney Roosters 22-16, before going down 24-18 to Brisbane. The inconsistency continued with a 20-18 victory over Newcastle being followed by a controversial 12-10 loss to St George-Illawarra. A bye in round seventeen left Canberra in eleventh place, but still within a win of the top eight.

In round 18, rookie winger James Schiller scored two tries as Canberra upset Melbourne 20-16. The Raiders then defeated NZ Warriors 26-14 with Corey Harawira-Naera crossing for two tries.

Nick Cotric and Sebastian Kris both scored doubles as Canberra defeated Gold Coast 36-24 to be in equal eighth place with five rounds to play.

A 26-6 loss to Penrith halted momentum, but Canberra bounced back to beat St George-Illawarra 24-22, and Newcastle 28-22 to keep their hopes alive. Centre Sebastian Kris scored two tries against the Knights.

In round 24, Canberra ran in nine tries, including a double from second row forward Hudson Young as they smashed Manly 48-6. The win was enough to put Canberra ahead of Brisbane in equal eighth place with one round to go.

After Brisbane went down to St George-Illawarra in the final round, all Canberra had to do was defeat Wests Tigers to secure an unlikely spot in the finals. They did that in style, scoring nine tries in a 56-10 mauling of the Tigers, who finished last. Hudson Young notched another double in the win.

Canberra finished in eighth place, and travelled to Melbourne for an elimination final. The Raiders had won their four previous encounters against the Storm in Melbourne, and made it five with a 28-20 upset victory.

The Raiders' season came to an end with a 40-4 monstering at the hands of Parramatta. Unlikely finalists a month out from the end of the regular season, Canberra could mark 2022 as a successful season despite the disappointing finish.

Sebastian Kris and Hudson Young were Canberra's leading try scorers for the season with fourteen each. The club's top point scorer was Jamal Fogarty with 116.

2023

Canberra retained the bulk of their 2022 squad that qualified for the finals. Fullback Charnze Nicoll-Klokstad left to join the New Zealand Warriors, while centre Semi Valemei moved to North Queensland midway through the season.

The Raiders began their season with a nail biting 19-18 loss to North Queensland; and followed up with a 20-14 loss to the new Redcliffe based Dolphins franchise.

In round three, Canberra played at home for the first time, and defeated Cronulla 24-20, thanks largely to two tries from Corey Horsburgh. Canberra then went down 24-14 to Newcastle, and were smashed 53-12 by defending premiers Penrith to sit in second last place after five rounds.

Canberra recovered to upset Brisbane 20-14, with winger Jordan Rapana scoring two tries. The Raiders beat St George-Illawarra 20-14 before picking up two points from a bye; and were back up to eleventh spot after eight rounds.

Canberra gained some payback on the Dolphins when a field goal from Jamal Fogarty secured a 31-30 golden point victory in Wagga Wagga. They followed up with an exciting 34-30 victory over Canterbury, with Jordan Rapana bagging a double.

In round eleven, Canberra defeated 2022 runners up Parramatta 26-18, and moved into the top eight. They held onto their spot despite a 42-14 mauling from Manly the following week.

Three tries from winger Albert Hopoate helped Canberra upset Souths 33-26 in round thirteen. They followed up with a lucky 20-19 escape over Wests Tigers thanks to two tries and a late penalty goal from Jamal Fogarty.

Canberra went down 36-14 to New Zealand Warriors before having another bye week. They stayed in the top eight with a tough 20-18 victory over Sydney Roosters, before beating Gold Coast 26-22, and St George-Illawarra 36-26. Centre Matthew Timoko scored two tries against the Dragons as Canberra were suddenly pushing for a top four spot.

A third bye week moved Canberra into the top four, but they fell back following a 21-20 golden point loss to the New Zealand Warriors. The Raiders lost 28-6 to Newcastle, before Sebastian Kris scored two tries to set up a 22-18 victory over the last placed Wests Tigers in round 23.

After suffering a humiliating 48-2 thrashing at the hands of Melbourne, Canberra ran in six tries in a 36-24 win over Canterbury which kept them in sixth place with two rounds to play.

In round 26, Canberra went down 29-18 to Brisbane, and found themselves needing to win their last round match to ensure their place in the finals. They were well beaten, 24-6 by Cronulla, but other results saw them manage to hang on to eighth place.

Canberra faced Newcastle in an elimination final. The Knights had won their last nine matches to storm into the finals, but Canberra led 16-6 at halftime. Newcastle fought back after the break, and the teams were locked at 28-28 at fulltime. In extra time, a penalty goal from Knights fullback proved the difference, and the 30-28 loss ended Canberra's season.

The Raiders may well look at 2023 as a replica of 2022; a successful result by making the finals, but disappointment at being unable to seriously threaten the top teams for the title.

A highlight of 2023 was club stalwart Jarrod Croker playing his 300th first grade game. Croker, who finished the season as Canberra's top point scorer with 130, announced his retirement. The Raiders' leading try scorers for the year were Matthew Timoko and Jordan Rapana, each with eleven.

2024

Canberra lost two of their most experienced backs with the retirement of Jarrod Croker, and the defection of Jack Wighton to South Sydney. Ricky Stuart put faith in his young players, such as Xavier Savage and Ethan Strange to fill the gaps, while they signed Manly utility Kaeo Weekes, and Penrith forward Zac Hosking.

Canberra began their season with a solid 28-12 away win over Newcastle, running in five tries. In their first game at home, the Raiders scored another five tries in a 32-12 victory over Wests Tigers. After going down 18-10 to the Warriors, Canberra lost 36-22 to Cronulla, and sat in the middle of the pack after four rounds.

In round five, Canberra scored seven tries, including a double from Matthew Timoko as they thrashed Parramatta 41-8. They followed up with a 21-20 golden point win over Gold Coast, thanks to a field goal from Jamal Fogarty. The result saw the Raiders move up to third spot.

A 34-10 loss to 2023 runners up Brisbane, and a shock 40-0 drubbing at the hands of Cronulla brought the Raiders back to earth. However in round nine, they came from well behind to snatch a 26-24 away win over Manly, with inspirational leader Elliott Whitehead bagging two tries. A bye in round ten saw Canberra inside the top eight.

New South Wales Origin forward Hudson Young scored two tries in a 24-20 win over Canterbury, before the Raiders fell 44-16 to Sydney Roosters. In round thirteen, Canberra secured an incredible 26-25 win over the Dolphins, when veteran Jordan Rapana kicked the first two field goals of his career.

After another bye week, Canberra fell 34-16 to North Queensland, 48-24 to Wests Tigers, and 16-6 to Melbourne to slump to twelfth place. The run of losses coincided with an injury to key halfback Jamal Fogarty.

After a hard fought 16-12 loss to Newcastle, and a third bye round, Canberra kept their finals hopes alive by eking out a 20-18 home win over the New Zealand Warriors. Hudson Young bagged another two tries in the win.

In round 21, Jordan Rapana scored two tries as Canberra made light work of Souths in a 32-12 victory which saw the Raiders move into ninth place, only behind the eighth placed Dolphins on for and against.

The following week, Canberra went down 22-18 to Canterbury as the Bulldogs celebrated a Back to Belmore weekend. A 46-24 home loss to manly followed, but the Raiders were still a win within the top eight with four rounds to play.

Canberra were their own worst enemy in a 42-4 shellacking at the hands of North Queensland in round 24. The loss left the Raiders needing to win at least two of their last three games, and hoping other results went their way.

The Raiders began their quest by upsetting three time defending premiers Penrith 22-18, with young winger Xavier Savage notching two tries. The following week, Canberra stayed alive by grinding out a 14-12 victory over the high flying Sydney Roosters. They went into the final round in a four way tie for eighth place, but had by far the worst four and against record of the contenders.

The season looked over when Canberra trailed early against St George-Illawarra; however they rallied in the second half to score an unlikely 26-24 win, thanks to a try from Corey Horsburgh in the final minutes, and a conversion from Kaeo Weekes. Unfortunately it wasn't enough to secure a spot in the finals, as Newcastle defeated the Dolphins the next day to secure the last spot in the finals.

Canberra finished in ninth place. Xavier Savage was the club's leading try scorer for the season with fifteen, while Jamal Fogarty topped their points scoring list with 90.

TOP POINT SCORERS

Jarrod Croker 2374
David Furner 1218
Clinton Schifcofske 1052
Mal Meninga 864
Gary Belcher 572
Ron Giteau 527
Jordan Rapana 496
Jason Croker 482
Laurie Daley 445
Brett Mullins 420
Terry Campese 345
Jack Wighton 300
Noa Nadruku 292
Phil Graham 292
Joel Monaghan 288
Jamal Fogarty 276
Chris O'Sullivan 273
Todd Carney 262
Mark McLinden 261
Luke Williamson 261
Josh Papali'i 256
Ruben Wiki 240
Nick Cotric 240
Ken Nagas 238
John Ferguson 200

TOP TRY SCORERS

Jarrod Croker 136
Jason Croker 120
Jordan Rapana 106
Brett Mullins 105
Laurie Daley 87
Jack Wighton 75
Mal Meninga 74
Noa Nadruku 73
Gary Belcher 69
Joel Monaghan 69
Phil Graham 68
Mark McLinden 65
Josh Papali'i 64
Chris O'Sullivan 62
Ruben Wiki 60
Nick Cotric 60
Ken Nagas 59
John Ferguson 50
David Furner 49
Craig Bellamy 46
Clinton Schifcofske 44
Elliott Whitehead 44
Reece Robinson 43
Hudson Young 43
Ashley Gilbert 41
Steve Walters 40

MOST GAMES

Jason Croker 318
Jarrod Croker 307
Josh Papali'i 305
Laurie Daley 245
Jack Wighton 242
Simon Woolford 234
Steve Walters 227
Ruben Wiki 224
Alan Tongue 220
Jordan Rapana 214
Elliott Whitehead 205
Ricky Stuart 203
Chris O'Sullivan 202
Dane Tilse 201
David Furner 200
Joseph Tapine 193
Brett Mullins 183
Brad Clyde 178
Luke Davico 176
Mal Meninga 166
Mark McLinden 165
Gary Coyne 159
Dean Lance 158
Troy Thompson 156
Craig Bellamy 149
Gary Belcher 148
Ken Nagas 142

Bibliography

Malcolm Andrews, "The ABC of Rugby League", Australian Broadcasting Corporation, 2006

Steve Haddan, "The Finals – 100 Years of National Rugby League Finals", Steven Haddan C/O QLD TV Limited, 2008

Alan Whiticker & Glen Hudson, "The Encyclopedia of Rugby League Players", Gary Allen Pty Ltd, 2007

Other material has come from a number of sources, including:

Big League

Rugby League Week

Sydney Morning Herald

The Daily Mirror, Sydney

The Daily Telegraph, Sydney

Some of the statistics have been obtained from www.rlstats.com

Printed in Great Britain
by Amazon

51885818R00106